CAREER METAMORPHOSIS:

Career Development Through Self-Understanding

By

Astrid Berg, M.S.

CAREER METAMORPHOSIS:
Career Development Through Self-Understanding

By Astrid Berg, M.S.

Copyright© 1990 SEFA BOOKS
P.O. Box 1686 Capitola, CA 95010

Library of Congress Cataloging in Publication Data
Berg, Astrid
Career Metamorphosis: Career Development through Self Understanding

ISBN - 0-9627862-7-6

Book Design, Typesetting & Graphics by Kasandra Fox, of:

Perfect Page Publishing

Santa Cruz, California 1990

ACKNOWLEDGMENTS

Thanks to my students: the young adults who come with dreams and enthusiasm, the re-entry people who bring depth and gratitude. In addition, thank you: Dick, for an inspiring career class; Barbara, for the encouragement to follow a dream; Linda and Barrie, for editing; Laura, for her personal support and for editing; Kasandra, for her skill and patience in typesetting and editing; Mildred, for her memory; my brother Danny, for his creative contribution; my parents, Anne and Anton, for believing in me; and to my son Sabin and husband Michael, for their patience throughout this process.

NOTE

The characters in this book are fictitious. Any resemblance to real persons, alive or deceased, is coincidental.

Exercises and advice offered in this book are designed to help the reader through the process of personal exploration and career decision-making. The author is not rendering counseling service through this book. If professional help is required, it is recommended that professional counseling be sought.

TABLE OF CONTENTS

(Continued)

CHAPTERS - Continued

PART TWO - MAJOR AND CAREER EXPLORATION

PART THREE - DYNAMICS OF JOB SEARCH

(Continued)

LIST OF TABLES

LIST OF FIGURES

EXERCISES

PART ONE - SELF ASSESSMENT

(C...

...orphosis

EXERCISES - Continued

PART TWO - MAJOR AND CAREER EXPLORATION

PART THREE - DYNAMICS OF JOB SEARCH

(Continued)

BIBLIOGRAPHY

Bear, John, *Bear's Guide to Earning Non-Traditional College Degrees*, 10th Ed. Berkeley: Ten Speed Press, 1988.

Bolles, Richard N., *What Color Is Your Parachute?* Berkeley: Ten Speed Press, 1980.

California State University, Long Beach *Catalog*, Vol. 39., No. 5, 1987.

Campbell, John, *The Portable Jung.* New York: Viking Press, 1971.

Careers. Ann Arbor: McGraw-Hill Publication, February, April/May, June, 1988.

Ekstrom, Ruth, Harris, Abigail and Lockheed, Marlaine, *How to Get College Credit for What You Have Learned as a Homemaker and Volunteer.* Princeton: Educational testing Service, 1982.

Erikson, Erik, *Childhood and Society.* New York: W.W. Norton, 1971.

Gelatt, H.B. "Information and Decision Theories Applied to College Choice," *Preparing School Counselors in Educational Guidance.* New York: College Entrance Examination Board, 1967.

Ginzberg, E., Ginsburg, S.W., Axelrad, S., and Herma, J.L., *Occupational Choice: An Approach to a General Theory.* New York: Columbia University Press, 1951.

Herr, Edwin L. and Cramer, Stanley H., *Career Guidance through the Life Span.* Boston: Little, Brown and Company, 1979.

Hirschorn, Michael W., "Students Over 25 Found to Make Up 45 Pct. of Campus Enrollments", *Chronicle of Higher Education*, March 30, 1988.

Holland, John H., *Making Vocational Choices: A Theory of Vocational Personalities and Work Environments* (Second edition). Englewood Cliffs: Prentice-Hall, 1985.

Josefowitz, Natasha, *Paths to Power: A Woman's Guide from First Job to Top Executive.* Reading: Addison-Wesley Publishing Company, 1986.

Levinson, D.J., et al, *The Seasons of a Man's Life.* New York: Alfred, Knopf, 1978.

Maslow, Abraham, *Motivation and Personality.* New York: Harper, 1954.

(Continued)

Maslow, Abraham, *The Further Reaches of Human Nature*. New York: Penguin Books, 1976.

Michelozzi, Betty Neville, *Coming Alive from Nine to Five* (Second edition). Palo Alto:, Mayfield Publishing Company, 1984.

Mitzel, Harold E. (ed.), *Encyclopedia of Educational Research*, Vol. 2, (5th Edition), New York: The Free Press, 1982.

National Education Association, *Higher Education Advocate*. February 1988.

Naisbitt, John and Aburdene, Patricia, *Megatrends 2000*. New York: William Morrow and Company, Inc., 1990.

Rancho Santiago College *Catalog*, 1986-87.

Sher, Barbara, *Wishcraft*. New York: Ballantine Books, 1979.

Super, Donald E., *Work Values Inventory*. Boston: Houghton Mifflin, 1970.

Super D.E., Starishesky, R., Matlin, N., and Jordaan, J.P., *Career Development Self-Concept Theory*. New York: College Entrance Board, 1963.

U.S. Department of Labor, *Dictionary of Occupational Titles* (Fourth edition). Washington D.C.: U.S. Government Printing Office, 1977.

U.S. Department of Labor, *Guide for Occupational Exploration*. Washington D.C.: U.S. Government Printing Office, 1984.

U.S. Department of Labor, *Occupational Outlook Handbook*. Washington D.C.: U.S. Government Printing Office, 1986-87.

Woolfolk, Anita E. *Educational Psychology* (Third edition). Englewood Cliffs: Prentice-Hall, 1985.

Zunker, Vernon G., *Career Counseling: Applied Concepts of Life Planning* (Second edition). Monterey: Brooks/Cole Publishing Company, 1986.

PREFACE

EVOLUTION OF
VOCATIONAL GUIDANCE

$\mathbf{P}$lanning for a career is not as simple and as predictable today as it was in the past. A series of economic and labor market changes have affected both the type of work we do and our concept of work. Science, technology, and demographics have played major roles in our employment trends.

Early in our history, we were a nation of farmers and through technological advancements evolved into an industrial economy. Nearing the twenty first century, science and technology has brought us into an information and service economy. The increasing number of women working outside of the home has had a major effect on the labor force. Orginally this increase was promoted by the event of World War II. It continued because of changed attitudes about women working and by more effective birth control methods.

Our concept of work has changed from a mere chore to an expression of ourselves. Our definitions of work are very different from those of our parents and grandparents. No longer is it the norm to find a life-long vocation. Instead career development has become a life-long process. On the average, we change our careers at least three times during our lives.

Prior to the industrial revolution workers were classified into: 1) the working class, or those who farmed, did crafts or provided services; and 2) professional class, such as, lawyers, teachers and high level clerks. The farmer and craftsman engaged in work which frequently included family members, and was performed near the home. Industrialization removed any satisfaction in work. Products were no longer personalized labors of love, and jobs became a means for earning wages to cover living expenses. Occupational choice was limited for all groups, and generally sons followed the vocations of their fathers while daughters married and ran households. Women who did work, were generally poor and did not choose their occupations; they worked out of financial necessity.

A result of the industrial revolution was the joining of the blue collar workers with the business and professional workers to comprise the middle class segment of our society. As industrialization and specialization created new jobs, and entire new fields, it became less usual for the sons (and daughters) of America to follow in their parents' foot steps.

As an outgrowth of the times, Frank Parsons, an engineer and labor reformist, developed a theory and process for individual career exploration. Before Parsons, the practice of palmistry (telling fortunes from lines on the palms of hands), phrenology (studying mental capacity from the conformations of the skull) and physiognomy (judging human characteristics from facial features) were the methods used for explaining occupational choice, if there was a choice at all. Frank Parsons also bridged the gap between school and the world of work. Parsons' work spurred the development of assessments for the classification and selection of personnel. In addition, vocational resources were published to describe different jobs. Frank Parsons' theory expanded into the development of numerous assessments, occupational information resources, and theories of career development. Yet all career development literature, including popular books on "figuring out what you want to do when you grow up", agree on Mr. Parsons' basic steps: Know yourself, know the world of work, and match the two.

CAREER SEARCH AND SELF-DISCOVERY

In studies of adult development, two factors stand out as the main threads in our lives: work and family. Today men work an average of forty years. Women with children spend an average of twenty-five years working outside of the home, while women without children spend an average of forty-five years at a job. Thus, career choices are of the most important decisions we make. Some individuals know exactly what they want to do. However, in the past decade, eighty percent of the working population were dissatisfied with their occupation. When many of these individuals made initial choices, they did not consider how their interests matched their career choices. Most often people just "fall into" their jobs without much forethought. Some individuals may have started in their field only as a temporary job, and never left because of financial necessity.

Many people expect to discover an answer to their career search from "tests" that will tell them what they are good at. Standardized assessments by themselves do not provide the answer. Assessments should be used as a means for further personal and career exploration. There is no magic wand. The answer to what you want to do when you grow up today is complex and takes in-depth self-exploration, a clear understanding of career options and patterns, as well as good self-management skills. The intent of this book is to provide the background theory for self-understanding as well as practical tools and techniques for identifying your career pattern.

PART ONE

SELF-ASSESSMENT

CHAPTER I:

INTRODUCTION

Are you unsure of what it is you want to do? Are you unhappy in your job? Would you like to find the perfect occupation for you? The key to finding out what career will suit you best is self-exploration. Uncovering who you are by understanding your values, interests, personality and skills is the first step to successful career development. By uncovering these parts of yourself, you will discover the core that is *YOU*. Just as life is a growth process, our work life is a developmental process. Jobs have become careers and our view of work is changing. We are looking for self expression and many of us seek this in our work.

Begin the self-exploration process by asking yourself these questions: How have I developed into the person I am now? What do I like and dislike? What is important to me in my life? What type of life style do I want to live? What am I seeking in a job? What are some of my personality traits? What skills do I have? What skills would I like to develop? What skills do I need to develop?

The task of this book, is to help you toward answering these questions. If this sounds like a sizable task, you are correct. It is also a necessary task that precedes exploring careers. It can be a rewarding endeavor, because the answers you find will bring you on a path to self-satisfaction.

Begin your personal exploration by going back to your childhood. Remember what it was you wanted to do before you were socialized to think differently, before you were told or you decided that you would not be good at it. We have a lot of *SHOULDS* in our lives. In order to know who you really are you need to get rid of the *SHOULDS* and find out what it is you really want. Once you have discovered your *core*, you can follow your history and see how and why it developed into what you are now. Were you encouraged to go with your dream? If so, by whom? If not, how did that make you change your mind about what you wanted to do or become? Who were the people that influenced and made an impression on you? What kinds of things happened in your growing up that made major effects on who you are now? Follow the steps you took, whether consciously or unconsciously, that led you to where you are now. Studying your personal history may also reveal clues about the development of your interests, personality, values and skills.

Understanding your interests and aptitudes will give you basic information about the general direction or directions you may choose to pursue. Skills come from interests and are developed because of successful experiences with these interests. Often we lose interest in the areas in which we were unsuccessful, and may prematurely disregard these early interests. Thus we do not develop skills in those areas to our actual potential. Interests and skills are also dependent on opportunity. Therefore, depth and breadth of experiences helps cultivate both interests and skills.

Your personality traits indicate what type of work environment suits you. This includes the types of people with whom you prefer to work, the actual physical surroundings and the type of activity you like to pursue. For instance, some people like to work alone, while others prefer to be surrounded by people. Some people like a structured environment, while others like looser guidelines. Some people like to work with tools or machines, while others may prefer numbers or words. Some of us may like repetitive tasks, while others need variety.

Your values are your motivators, and indicate what it is you will need in order to be happy and successful at work, and in your life in general. Not all of us are motivated by the same things. Some of us like challenge, while others are motivated by security. Some of us may choose to help society, while others become thrilled with the opportunity to travel. Combining the four factors, values, interests, skills and personality is the self-assessment portion of your venture.

After discovering yourself, you will investigate what types of opportunities are available for someone with your special qualifications. Most of us have a vague idea of the many kinds of occupations that exist. Usually we have a misconception about what people do in their jobs because we get our ideas from a thirty-minute television series, or brief connections with people in different jobs. It is difficult to stay current with the changes in the world of work.

I will discuss some of these trends, and sources for information on the careers you are exploring. It will be important for you to explore opportunities extensively, and consider any and all options. Frequently, we discard occupational choices because we think they may be too difficult to enter, that our skills are not good enough, or that it will take too much time to get there. Explore before you decide. Talk to several people in that occupation. Also investigate related occupations. The more information you have the better decision you will be able to make. And only then, are you ready to make a decision.

Because you have already extensively analyzed who you are, the task of decision-making is a natural outcome of your personal and career explorations. To be effective at decision-making you must compromise and prioritize the different aspects and desires of your personal and work life. Once you have made your decision, you will need to motivate, organize, and prepare to reach the goal you have set. Setting goals is a key to your success. And lastly, knowing the techniques for active and positive job search will help you land that perfect job for you. So, are you ready?

INTRODUCING THE SMITH FAMILY

MIKE, ANNE, SEAN and **MARY** are members of the Smith family who will serve as role models in the career exploration process. The family lives in a middle class suburban area in America with the father, Mike, being the chief bread winner. Many changes have occurred since Mike and Anne attended college in the sixties. Their children, Sean and Mary, are in college.

Mary, the daughter, has borrowed some of her mother's relics from the sixties to wear to a party. Mary, a freshman is considering a major in English, but is unsure about the job possibilities with a liberal arts degree. Mary is very conscientious, yet has never felt that she was good at anything. Somewhat of an introvert, she was only mildly involved in high school activities and has had little exposure to the opportunities available to her. She is creative and a dreamer. She expresses herself with clothes, and in her journal. Because she is rather inhibited, Mary does not show her writing to others.

The son, Sean is very outgoing. In high school he was involved in sports, the debate team, and several clubs. His history teacher's comment is, "Sean has the potential to do much better, but he's too busy socializing." Sean entered college undeclared, but decided to major in business because he would like a job working for a big company and have a fancy office. Sean's problem is that he's not focusing on his education. Although he is in his third year of college, he has not completed the courses he will need in order to graduate by his senior year. Sean's priorities are recreation, socializing, and his job at the stereo shop.

Since her children have been in college, Anne has felt both exuberant and empty. She enrolled in a beginning computer class and aerobic class at the local community college. She is thinking about returning to the work force. Anne was the kind of mother who participated in all the children's activities — she was always there to support teams, make projects, give rides, etc. Anne was also involved in the P.T.A., church and several local charitable organizations. Anne's hobby is collecting antiques. She has thought about opening her own business, but is not confident that she could successfully run a business. She has also thought about working in a real estate office and eventually obtaining her license to go into sales. Anne met her husband in college and married before she finished her degree in history.

Mike began working for the city at about the same time he married Anne. His major in college was biology. He was particularly interested in wildlife biology, but at the time, he wasn't motivated to attend graduate school. Unable to find interesting work in his field, Mike took a job with the city planning department and has been there for twenty years. Mike usually enjoys his job. Now that his children are becoming independent, he no longer feels the weight of being the family provider. He is a little envious of his wife who has the freedom to take fun classes and do what she likes. Mike is not considering a career change, yet he is ready for some kind of change. He teases his wife about her getting a job to support him so he can stay home.

EXERCISE 1 - PERSONAL INVENTORY

1.   Childhood fantasy: What are some of the things you wanted to be when you were a kid?

2.   Who was your hero or heroine? Role model?

3.   What is your job now?

4.   What do you like about your job? If unemployed, about your last job?

5.   What don't you like about your current (or last) job?

6.   What do you think you might like to do: Practical/logical? Explorative/fanciful?

7.   What general field of work seems interesting to you?

8.   What is your best skill?

9.   What skill would you like to acquire or improve upon?

10.   Complete sentence: The purpose of work is . . .

11.   How many years of education are you willing to pursue? To what degree?

12.   What do you want from a job?

13.   What kind of life-style do you seek?

14.   Describe yourself in five words.

15.   What types of people do you like to be around?

The exercises in this book are designed to help you discover your interests, skills, personality and values and match them to occupations. Once you have completed all of Part One on self-understanding, turn to Chapter 8, *Exercise 13 - The Personal Exploration Summary,* which is a summary of all your self exploration execises. In Part Two of this book you will explore educational possibilities, research occupations that best fit you, and set some goals. In Part Three you learn job search techniques. Throughout the book are examples of how the Smith Family completed the assignments.

CHAPTER TWO:

CAREER
DEVELOPMENT PROCESS

Don't be alarmed if you are unable to answer with confidence the proposed questions in the previous chapter. If you knew the answers, you would not need this book.

Be sure to realize that understanding yourself is a process in which you uncover bit by bit as you are growing, changing and maturing. Your persona is not static. Some of your answers now will be different than they were ten years before, and will change ten years from now. We often enter "adulthood" assuming there is little growth, and only a few changes. It is only recently that psychologists have studied adult development and that the popularity of "self-help" books is widespread.

Understanding your own development (as both child and adult) will disclose the answers to your questions and uncover your potential. I will introduce Erik Erikson's theory of human development and the Ginzberg, Ginsburg, Axelrad and Herma theory of career development, as a basis for reviewing and understanding yourself. Tables 1, 2 and 3 outline the stages of development by theorist. I make references to additional theorists whose works are included in the bibliography.

CHILDHOOD

Erik Erikson is known for his theories on human development, particularly child development. Erikson emphasizes the relationship between culture and the individual's emotional needs. He proposed that both internal and external factors mold us. He identified eight stages of development from infancy to old age. Each stage involves a central crisis that we must resolve. Adequate resolution leads to personal and social competence and a stronger foundation for resolving future crises. Inadequate resolution impedes future growth and will result in repeated crises occurring around the unresolved issue.

In the first stage, *Trust vs. Mistrust,* as infants we depend on our parents to respond to our basic needs. Consistency in our environment is important in order for us to trust. *Autonomy vs. Shame and Doubt* begins at approximately one year of age, when we become mobile. As toddlers, we need to explore and master our environment and assume some responsibility, such as, feeding and toileting. When we are not allowed to be autonomous, we will doubt our ability to do so and feel ashamed because we are not capable. Parents need to balance between protecting children and providing the freedom to learn. At preschool age we enter *Initiative vs. Guilt.* At this stage, we need confirmation that our initiative is accepted and valued. For instance, the child who wants to help prepare dinner, or fix a toy that is broken is expressing an interest to do something on his own. At this stage we are also torn between what we want to do and what we should do. We learn to balance the desire to act on impulse with the basic rules of the household, such as, not touching the stereo.

By school age, we are eager to engage in productive work, and can begin to realize and appreciate the relationship between perseverance and completing a task. We need to believe in ourselves and know that we are competent. Erikson calls this *Industry vs. Inferiority* because we learn about achievement and failure. A child who is successful and rewarded for industry will develop a positive self-image. The child who is unsuccessful and experiences failure will feel inferior. I will discuss the remainder of Erikson's stages in the sections on adolescence and adulthood.

According to career developmental theorists such as Ginzberg, Ginsburg, Axelrad and Herma (1951), vocational development occurs throughout our lives. Stages of development are based on the physical maturation process. The environment also influences development and career choices, and provides us with role models for our initial choices.

We begin our career exploration with a *Fantasy* stage in which we imagine what we would like to be when we grow up. For instance, Anne wanted to be a princess. Children pretend and act out the occupations of their fantasy, like when Anne pretended that she was Snow White. In these first stages, children play at their fantasies because they enjoy it, because it feels good, and because it is fun. As they become more socialized and seek adult approval they may fantasize occupations that are similar to their role models, such as parents, other family members, and teachers. For instance, when Anne was six, she wanted to be a nurse like her aunt.

We move into a *Tentative* stage around puberty. Career choices are now based on a broader perspective. We become more exposed to the world, we begin to understand the concept of work, and we begin to realize our interests and skills. Our career choices are no longer modeling our parents, close family or favorite television heroes, but extend to other members of the community. For example, after playing a few years of little league baseball and identifying with baseball heroes, like Reggie Jackson, Sean wanted to become a professional ball player, or a coach. During the Tentative Period we also recognize that we are better at some things than at others and relate our aptitudes to particular occupations.

For instance, Mike realized that he had skills in mathematics and interest in science, and considered the occupations in the sciences. On the other hand, Anne was pretty good at drawing but didn't think her mathematics was good enough to become an architect. Children need role models to encourage them to pursue their interests.

Typically, girls with high level math and science skills are not encouraged to become doctors or engineers, but rather, nurses and science teachers. Boys may not be encouraged to pursue an interest in the arts or dance because these occupations are viewed as feminine. Exposing children to role models from both sexes, and their own racial, ethnic and cultural groups offers the encouragement needed to pursue their dreams. The exploration of career alternatives helps to expose young people to opportunities, and with proper guidance, can motivate them to realize their full potential. The *Tentative* stage continues throughout adolescence and the latter part of this stage will be discussed in the section on adolescence.

ADOLESCENCE

The concerns over adolescent issues such as teen pregnancy, drug and alcohol abuse, AIDS, popular music and popular trends (hippie, skin head or punk movements) is rampant. Adolescence is a turbulent period for most of us. Many major life and career decisions come to focus at this time — a time when we are evaluating so many personal issues.

Adults worry and complain about the actions of each new generation. Today's world is not less moral, only more complex. With numerous choices regarding life-style, careers, college majors, marriage and children, it is much more difficult for our youth today. We usually do not have the information and resources to make these choices. With freedom or free choice comes a great deal of responsibility. It's a facile task to choose between staying on the farm, or moving to town to work for your uncle, compared to deciding whether or not to attend college, what to study, what to do instead of college. The pace of society is much faster and our influences are global. It is difficult to keep up with the new trends and to comprehend what a career may entail when the job requirements may change before we graduate from college. As a result, parents, teachers, and counselors have an all encompassing task in guiding and advising youth. And frequently, parents and even counselors, are not prepared for this task. Today, simple college orientation courses have evolved into career and life planning courses that are not only popular but a necessity for college survival.

The major issues that confront adolescents are sexuality, identity, values, sex roles, self-concept, moral development, education/career decisions, and peer relations. The resolution of these issues is a cardinal point in our lives with the outcome bringing forth significant consequences. According to Erikson, the developmental stage during this period is *Identity vs. Role Diffusion*. We are breaking into the adult world, and moving from dependent child to becoming our own person. In seeking our identities, we may latch on to another person, as in a boy or girl friend, or a group, as in a peer group or gang, to provide that identity. The desire to be accepted by peers is very powerful for an adolescent. Sexual identity, or better described as recognition for our sexual attractiveness, is a significant part of peer acceptance. However, sexual development encompasses responsibilities. For the young woman it is the ability to bear children, and for the young man it is the initiation into traditional male role of provider. The desire to be sexually attractive, as well as active, is reinforced by the media and our peers, whereas moral messages say that sex is for marriage only. Thus, we see conflicts in our environment that are magnified by our inner conflicts.

In addition, attachment to a group or a person does not allow us to discover and develop our own individuality. Hence, we find women whose identity comes from their association with their husbands. This happened to Anne, who had developed some interest in her education and career, yet had not settled on a role for herself. She was more confused by the new attitudes of the sixties, and chose to follow the path of her own mother. She married Mike before completing her education and within a year Sean was born. At that time her identity was as a wife and mother.

When her children became more independent, she again, became confused because her role as a mother was changing. She had not developed a personal identity aside from her roles as homemaker and wife.

During the latter part of adolescence we enter the stage of *Intimacy vs. Isolation*. The major task of this period is to relate with another human being on a personal and deeper level. Intimate means private, personal, close, deep and thorough. In order to be intimate, we need to feel confident and comfortable with ourselves. Mary had a steady boy friend for her last two years of high school, but upon entering college she found that she was not only confused about her future educational and career goals, but was unsure about her feelings for her boy friend. So, she decided to break up with him.

As part of shaping our identities we need to explore our values, interests, skills and personality. We are confronted with several views from our culture, religion, parents, peer groups, teachers, and leaders. This makes it difficult to develop our own views. According to Ginzberg, during adolescence we become aware of how occupations affect life styles, and how our life styles may influence the occupations we choose. Mike chose not to become a wild life biologist because he wanted to be home to raise his family. He compromised his interest in wildlife for his value of family. Anne compromised, as well, by choosing to stay at home with her children rather than continuing with her education.

At the end of high school we enter a *Transition* stage, during which we decide on college, and/or occupations. Ginzberg's theory continues with the *Realistic* stage, which begins upon entering college. During this time, we explore occupations, college majors, and life styles. When we find something we like, it's called *Crystallization*. Often, after entering a particular major, or trying an occupation, we find that it is not what we had anticipated, or what Ginzberg calls *Psuedo-Crystallization*. For example, Sean chose business because it was a major that related to his interest and he thought it would guarantee him a high paying job. However, Sean does not enjoy the courses in his major and would like to quit school altogether.

In some cases, further exploration is necessary to make a new decision. Once we are assured of our decision, we specialize in a field, which is called *Specification*. For instance, Mary is exploring careers in writing. She may specify her choice by becoming a journalist, or she may enter a graduate program in creative writing. The last stage of this period is *Implementation* and occurs when we begin a job in our field.

As you can see, personal growth issues are interwoven with career development issues. The stages of career development do not occur as orderly and effortlessly as described in theory. They do not occur in absence of emotional and psychological development. To understand this development, we must ask ourselves: Have we been encouraged over the years? To what types of subjects and information on occupations have we been exposed? What personal issues affect our choices? These factors will strongly influence our career development and choices. We all go through these basic steps in one form or another, and our growth and self-understanding often continue into adulthood.

ADULTHOOD

Entering adulthood does not mean that opportunity for growth and development has passed. As youths we tend to think that adulthood consists of work, marriage and family, and that life sort of continues with no real milestones other than having children and becoming grandparents. There are as many adjustments, changes and learning processes during the remaining forty to seventy years of our lives as in the first twenty. We are overcoming the unresolved childhood conflicts while we handle all the adult responsibilities, choices and tasks.

With the complexity of modern society and very little education on how to handle or cope with these situations, the process can be overwhelming. It can also be challenging and rewarding. Psychologists propose different theories on adult development, some involving conflicts, as Erikson's theory, others involving stages based on age gradients, and others based on specific tasks to be completed from stage to stage. I will continue with Erikson's conflicts to provide you with one solid theoretical basis of human development. Instead of discussing other theorists separately, I combine their thoughts on developmental processes typically encountered by most of us.

BECOMING AN ADULT: Becoming an adult is the transition period in which we no longer are considered children, yet are not quite adults. Today, this stage is extended into the twenties because many of us remain dependent on our parents while attending college. During this time, we make several decisions and fill many roles. We are still seeking our identities. We usually make decisions regarding educational or occupational choices. Those of us who attend college are exploring and changing majors. Those of us who are not attending college are trying out jobs.

According to Sarason (1977), the process of choosing careers is done with the expectation that our choices will determine how we fill in the rest of our lives. With the variety of choices and the pressures placed on students to narrow their choices, as is frequently required by educational system, we often make them when we are not ready. Because we consider choices as life long commitments, we have great difficulties in deciding. As a result, we often begin a lifetime in a field which is usually not our first, second or even third choice.

Choosing an occupation is not the only issue of this period. We are frequently still in the midst of Erikson's *Intimacy vs. Isolation.* Interacting with members of the opposite sex may be a strong stimulus, or the only one. For instance, women have traditionally been socialized to set their primary goals on marriage, even when they plan to have a career. All of Anne's friends were wed straight out of high school, and Anne quit college to get married. Although not as common, that is still the norm with today's generation.

Our late teens and early twenties are also periods for seeking independence from our parents, both financially and emotionally. With so many things to work out, it all seems complicated and we just want to know what is ahead of us. We don't want to think about it, because this should be the time to enjoy the freedom of finally being an adult and getting to do what we want. We find, instead, that there are more rules, and more reasons to wait (delayed gratification). Those of us who are working clock in and out, and are always accountable for our time. As college students, we take many classes we don't like, plus the homework has tripled since high school. Parents want us to do something practical and secure. We want to be rock stars, airplane pilots, writers, or wildlife biologists.

We get through the years sometimes having a lot of fun along the way, not sure how we got out of college, or not sure how the years of punching in and out went by so fast. We have changed our majors or jobs a few times. We have had some serious relationships, and may have found that special person. We have somehow learned how to be responsible for ourselves. Some of us have made some major decisions about who we are, and are working toward our goals. But, most of us have fallen into our jobs because it was too confusing to figure it all out.

ADULTHOOD: This closely approximates Erikson's stage of *Generativity vs. Stagnation.* While *generativity* often refers to raising children or providing for the next generation, it also implies a broader meaning of giving back to society or making an impact on the community. *Stagnation* is the feeling that we have nothing to contribute.

By our mid to late twenties we are usually married and are considering, or have started a family. Our friends and family expect us to have a stable job/career by now. We have now "made it into the adult world" and acquire possessions like microwaves, V.C.R.'s, compact disk players, pets and homes. We hear our own parents' words when talking to our children. Life can be very satisfying because we are actualizing some of our goals, because we make and act upon some major decisions, and because we are responsible, respected and independent.

We may be unhappy with our early decisions regarding marriage, work, children and/or life-style. If by the late twenties to early thirties we haven't found our niche, or are dissatisfied with our original choices, we are in what Daniel Levinson (1977) calls "the Age Thirty Transition". I would not put an age limitation on this transition because it may happen any time during early adulthood, and is dependent on many outside factors. Divorce and unemployment will serve as catalysts for this transition period. Transition is a time for assessing our early life decisions and for making some changes.

This happened to Mike. At thirty he was bored with his job, but could see no way out. He didn't want to start all over in a new career, and Anne couldn't work because of the children. He made some small adjustments in his life, such as, taking up fishing.

The same thing happened to Anne a few years later. When the children were in school, she became restless and unsure of her new role. She picked up a part time job as a library clerk. Although it was never verbalized, because the Smiths viewed themselves as a modern family, the kids and Mike were resentful. Things around the house became disorganized. Anne was distracted at work and found that her job wasn't as gratifying as she had hoped. They didn't need her income, so within a year she quit. Soon after, she began to collect antiques.

Life after thirty continues with more changes. We adjust to marriage and family life, and we become involved in our communities, we grow and advance at work, we pick up hobbies or other activities within or outside of the home, and we begin to gain some status. We may be actualizing some of our internal values whether they are humanitarian, achievement oriented, or materialistic.

For some people, the outlook is not as positive, and either life at home, at work, or both seem unbearable. Some of us stick with it, even though we are unhappy, and others make changes in jobs or careers, or dissolve marriages. Many of us are also adjusting to the aging of our parents and children, and the role reversals that may be occurring. These roles and adjustments continue into our forties.

MID-LIFE: This period has been researched, discussed, analyzed and publicized more than any other stage in adulthood. The idea of a mid-life crisis denotes that something negative will happen, which is not at all accurate.

Much of what happens during this period, depends on our internal lives, such as previous decisions, fulfilled or unfulfilled goals, family changes (kids growing, divorce, death), employment status, as well as external influences, such as our culture, the nation's economy and its political position. Most social scientists agree that this is a period of looking inward and reflecting. Carl Jung calls it "the noon of life". Levinson describes the mid-life transition period as a strong amount of questioning about the basis of life, the need to affirm self by society through success in career, and the realization and acceptance of differences between early goals and present achievement.

Resulting career changes are a dramatic horizontal move from one career to another, or a vertical advancement within our career to levels of managerial or supervisory responsibilities. Motivations for these changes can be environmental (lay off), family (children leaving home), or self (search for greater satisfaction).

The task of mid-life transition is to reassert our control over our self-development and to become active in controlling our future rather than passively following a course of action that was set in motion years before.

At this stage, we also begin to notice our energy level is not as high as it used to be. We tend to notice people who are younger than ourselves. Our children's teachers seem too young to be out of school themselves. Store clerks may call us "sir" or "ma'am". Some of our friends may have minor ailments, or even serious illnesses. Our parents are retired, in convalescent homes, or have passed away. Our children have minds of their own, or are on their own. We think about where we have been and how did time pass so quickly. We start talking to God, or reassessing the meaning of it all. This is the period to evaluate and prepare for the second half of our lives.

Both Anne and Mike are at this point. Mike realizes that his next promotion will only come if the head of the department dies or retires. In order for Mike to advance, he will have to make a lateral move to a different department, or change companies. He is not sure that he wants to do any of the above. Anne is confused. With the children in college, she feels released from major responsibilities. On the other hand, she is fearful of the unknown. This is the first time she has had the time and leisure to think only of herself. She is not sure how to do that. She also misses being needed.

LATE ADULTHOOD: In American culture we typically do not respect those in later adulthood. As old folks, we lose status with our children, and possibly at work. Our doctors remind us to eat right and to exercise. More friends are getting ill. Some friends are retiring. Other friends may return to school, take up hobbies, or start new jobs. Our parents may have passed on. We want respect, to be independent and to have our loved ones around us. We want to understand the changing world, and have others listen to how it was. We become concerned about death and the after-life, and about being alone.

With the advancing age of the baby boom generation we are seeing a major increase in the median age of adults. Advancements in the medical sciences have dramatically increased our life spans. Our attitudes must change, because soon those over fifty will be in the majority.

This period refers to Erikson's *Integrity vs. Despair*. Achieving integrity means integrating and accepting our past and ourselves. When unable to attain a feeling of fulfillment and completeness from our lives we will sink into despair. To achieve Erikson's integrity we can look upon this period of life as an opportunity to continue to make contributions in a less traditional manner than through work. For instance, retired adults can give back to society in a charitable manner, or take on a new interest whether it be vocational or avocational.

CONCLUSION: The descriptions above may not fit you or your family's life-style. Most research in human development is based on a white, middle class population. Until research more accurately describes all populations we only have this information to use. In any case, we all must consider that changes will occur throughout our lives. Some of these changes will be due to the physical aging process, and others to emotional aging, or maturity. I call this the internal development, which includes aspects such as our basic personality, our physical condition, previous experiences as children and adults, our personal philosophy of life, how we have made adjustments to the negatives in our lives, and our personal relationships with others.

However, much of our development is effected by external factors, over which we have varying degrees of control. Most of these factors have to do with our environment and socialization, such as our religion, the state of the economy or our socio-economic group. Other specific external factors are timing of marriage and children, divorce, loss of spouse, and unemployment. Thus, adult developmental stages are influenced by natural growth and maturation, as well as environmental and situational conditions.

EXCERCISE 2 - CHILDHOOD FANTASY

Think back on your life and remember some of your childhood fantasies. What did you want to be? Anne, after watching a movie set in beautiful southern mansion with looming staircases, drew floor plans. Mary read novels about horses and wanted to be a jockey. Mike, after watching his dog have puppies, wanted to be a veterinarian. Sean wanted to be a famous athlete. Did you act out on your fantasies?

Now remember your school days. What was your favorite subject? Who was your favorite teacher? What was special about that person? Did your favorite classes change as you became older? If so, do you remember what made them change? Were you usually good at what you liked? Was there anything you liked doing that you felt you didn't do well? Were you ever told that you couldn't do something well? Who told you that? Did you believe them? Could you have become better with practice and encouragement? Write down a couple of the fantasy occupations, favorite subjects, remembered teachers and so on. Include your favorite fantasy on your Personal Exploration Summary.

EXERCISE 3 - AUTOBIOGRAPHY

Write a one to three page autobiography. Describe your experiences with both Erikson's and Ginzberg's developmental stages. (See Smith Family example on upcoming pages.)

SMITH FAMILY

Exercise 3 - Autobiography

MIKE:

One of my first memories was of my mother screaming at the sight of my closet. I had been collecting rocks, bones, leaves, anything I could find, and pigeon-holing them. My mom told me to keep my collections outside. It didn't stop me from collecting. I just became neater and my collections were less obtrusive. I also brought home strays. My first was a caterpillar. I kept it in a jar with holes poked in the lid, and watched the caterpillar turn into a cocoon and then into a moth. I didn't want to let it go. I distinctly remember my dog, Lady, having puppies. I didn't want to give those away either. (This was Ginzberg's *Fantasy Stage*.) I wanted to be a vet and an animal breeder.

When I became older, the neighborhood kids played war games, sports and things like that. Later we would protest these "war games." School didn't have any major pull (Erikson: *Industry vs. Inferiority*), except for my science classes because I liked dissecting (Ginzberg: *Tentative - Interest and Skill*). As teenagers, we fell into the typical things of the times. I guess I was of a hippie persuasion. There were a lot of conflicts between myself and my father over my hair, my music, my friends, my behavior, my political beliefs — the typical scene of the times. My parents divorced during that time. I suppose I was angry at my dad for leaving my mom. Although, it turned out to be the best thing for her. According to Erikson, I was finding my identity.

In college I was into saving the environment. (Ginzberg: *Realistic - Exploration and Crystallization*). But when I graduated, there weren't paying jobs for that kind of thing. Even biologists with Ph.D's were struggling for research funds.

After Anne and I were married, I obtained a CETA job with the city doing some basic demographic research (Ginzberg: *Realistic - Specification*). I found it pretty interesting, and chalked off wildlife biology as a kid's fantasy. Other things became important, like my family, and getting ahead. I slowly let go of many of my previously close-held hippie values. I've been pretty lucky in my job. It has been financially rewarding — Anne really never had to work. (Erikson: *Generativity vs. Stagnation*). I also enjoy my colleagues, most of whom are friends. We all started

(Continued)

SMITH FAMILY - Continued

there straight out of college. It's hard to believe that I have actually been there twenty years. It's only since the kids have gone to college, and Anne is going through her mid-life crisis that I also begin to wonder. My reasons for being at work are gone. I would like to rekindle some of the values I have ignored because of conflicting motivations. I would like to be more challenged in my job, or should I say, differently challenged? But do I really want a change? I'm not sure. I guess this is mid-life.

SMITH FAMILY - Continued

ANNE:

I loved watching movies. Shirley Temple was my favorite movie star. I was more interested in the grand houses with the banister, the rugs, the furniture, than with Shirley's roles. After watching a movie, my imagination went wild. I would draw imaginary houses (they were actually floor plans) and would fantasize living in them. My fantasy occupation, if I had known what to call it then, was to be an architect (Ginzberg: *Fantasy*). Around puberty, I became more interested in the furnishings of houses, and must admit I had the "coolest" room of all my friends (Ginzberg: *Interests and Skills*). During my teens I was an avid Beatle fan. I was a cheerleader. I was intrigued with the happenings of the sixties, but was prudent and conservative. I'm glad I went to college because it really opened my mind (Ginzberg: *Values/Life Styles*). I was raised pretty conservatively, and I can remember being embarrassed when a professor would show us how isolated we had been. He talked to us about civil rights, homosexuality, poverty, war. My husband, or boyfriend at the time, also changed the way I thought. My parents were against me seeing him. Now that I look back, part of my interest in him was a rebellion, and, in part it was finding out about myself. All of this would relate to Erikson: *Identity vs. Role Diffusion*.

Deciding on a college and then attending college was done with little foresight or planning. I was basically interested in socializing and boys. In college I majored in history because it was my best subject in high school (Ginzberg: *Exploration*). I thought about teaching because that's the kind of thing women did (this was in the very early stages of bra burning). I did very little exploration before I became pregnant, and then I quit school (Erikson: *Intimacy vs. Isolation* took precedence over *Identity vs. Role Diffusion*). However, this was how things went in my social circles. Most of my friends were marrying and having children. Raising my children was rewarding enough most of the time (Erikson: *Generativity vs. Stagnation*). There were times when I longed to be part of the world of work, but to tell you the truth, I couldn't imagine having had time to go to work. When I did try it, I found my life a shambles (a mini age-thirty transition). It wasn't really worth it. I do have to admit that I sometimes envied my husband. When my mother died of cancer, I immersed myself in my family even more. It felt safe.

(Continued)

SMITH FAMILY - Continued

In looking back, I see the stagnation of the last five or so years (Erikson: *Generativity vs. Stagnation*). With the kids pretty much on their own, I feel it is my turn now. I don't know what I want to do, but I do feel more confident. I've been collecting and restoring antiques, but I think I should keep it as a hobby and do something practical.

I could go back to teaching. There is a demand, if they would hire anyone my age. I also think it would be nice to work in an office, with adults. I thought about real estate, because I like homes and am good with people. I guess I am re-exploring my career options and am in the middle adult, or mid-life transition stage.

SMITH FAMILY - Continued

SEAN:

As a kid, I wanted to be the usual things: a famous athlete, an actor, a fireman (Ginzberg: *Fantasy*). I don't see how any of that relates to now, except that I like being in front of a crowd and I was good at it (Ginzberg: *Tentative - Interest and Skill*). In my high school speech class I was the only one who wasn't nervous. I would always do crazy things. I did a lot of things in high school, like ski club, water polo, and organized dances (Erikson: *Industry vs. Inferiority*). I can't see how any of that applies to a job.

I want to be around people; I don't want to be stuck in an office. I thought of being a salesman because they make money and set their own hours (Ginzberg: *Tentative - Life Style*). I work at an electronics store right now and do pretty good. I thought if I get a degree in business, it would be something I could fall back on.

I don't want to make the wrong career decision. I don't really know what else I could get into (Ginzberg: *Realistic - Exploration*). I would also like to move out of the house and be financially independent. I am not real sure if college is for me. It's the thing you do after high school (Ginzberg: *Transition*). Right now, I'm at the tail end of adolescence and in the early stages of becoming an adult, because I am making some adult decisions and paying half my own way.

SMITH FAMILY - Continued

MARY:

I liked horses. I read Walter Farley. When the *Black Stallion* movie came out, I was about twelve. I wanted to be a jockey. Even before I could read, I was always pretending to be animals (Ginzberg: *Fantasy*). I tease my dad by saying I had this need to be an animal because he prefers them over people. My fantasy stage continued until high school, where I did as I had before in school — my best, which was OK but not impressive. Maybe I was stuck in Erikson's *Inferiority* stage because I did not excel like my brother did . . . until Mr. Russell. No teacher has motivated me (role model) as much as this English teacher. I felt successful in his class (Erikson: *Industry vs. Inferiority*), and I freely explored my interests and talents (Ginzberg: *Interest and Skill*). Unfortunately, he left after the first semester. I thought I wanted to be a writer. When we looked up occupations in high school, I realized how difficult it would be to make a living at writing. Was I still stuck in *Inferiority* (Erikson) or being realistic about my skills (Ginzberg: *Tentative*)? Erikson's *Identity vs. Role Diffusion* comes about now: I also thought about fashion design or merchandising, but now that I work in a clothing store, I figure that isn't for me either. In high school I didn't follow any particular crowd. I usually watched them. I like figuring people out, so I thought about psychology. But I'm not the kind of person people come to for advice, so maybe I'd never get clients. I'm exploring majors, careers and identity right now (Both Ginzberg: *Exploration* and Erikson: *Identity vs. Role Diffusion*). I am also testing *Intimacy vs. Isolation* (Erikson): who will like me for me?

TABLE 1 - CHILDHOOD STAGES OF DEVELOPMENT

ERIKSON:

Trust vs. Mistrust	Autonomy vs. Shame & Doubt	Initiative vs. Guilt	Industry vs. Inferiority
Parental Trust	Mobility	Spontaneous	Responsible
Parental Distrust	Over-Protected	Rigid	Irresponsible
Comfort	Secure	Motivated	Able
Discomfort	Insecure	Apathetic	Unable
Basic Needs Are Met	Independent	Desire	Competent
Basic Needs Are Not Met	Dependent	Fault	Inadequate
		Want	Success
		Should	Failure

GINZBERG:

Fantasy	Tentative: Interest	Tentative: Capacity
Intrinsic Play	Likes	Best Subject
Extrinsic Play	Dislikes	Worst Subject
Family Model	Community Model	Ability
Playing	Preferences	Aptitude

TABLE 2 - ADOLESCENT STAGES OF DEVELOPMENT

ERIKSON:

Identity vs. Role Diffusion	Intimacy vs. Isolation
Individuality	Friendship
Roles	Loneliness
Integrity	Belonging
Confusion	Separation
Peer Acceptance	Relationships
Deviate	Withdrawal
Independence	Social Group

GINZBERG:

Tentative Values	Transition	Realistic: Exploration
Life-Style	College	Majors
Work-Style	Occupation	Internship/Career
First Work Experience	Future	Crystallization
		Pseudo-Crystallization
		Financial Independence

TABLE 3 - ADULT STAGES OF DEVELOPMENT

ERIKSON:

Generativity vs. Stagnation	Integrity vs. Despair
Extroverted	Introverted
Create Life Structure	Review Life Values
Home and Family	Increased Leisure
First Career	Career Peak
Confirm Career	Retirement
Making It	Loss of Youth and Status
Finding Niche	Leaving Something Behind
Balance of Life Expectations	Limited Time

GINZBERG:

Realistic: Specification	Realistic: Implementation
Field of Study	Resume
Specify	Interview
Set Goals	Graduate School
	First Career

CHAPTER III:

PERSONALITY

You have begun the self assessment process by remembering when you were young and when you had fantasies of things you would like to do. Meanwhile, you have grown up and have let go of your old dreams. In order to look at who you are today, and to remember some of who you once were, you will need to combine self exploration exercises with objective assessments.

First you will explore your personality. In the Personal Inventory exercise I asked you to describe yourself. I want you to think about what is unique about you. What special characteristics do you have? What can you add to a work environment? Knowing the type of person you are and how you fit into the the world of work will help you to decide on a general field. That is the goal of this chapter.

What is personality?The dictionary describes personality as "the dynamic character, self or psyche that constitutes and animates the individual person and makes his experience of life unique." Our personality is the behavior, temperamental, emotional and mental expression of who we are. It is an expression of our core.

Why must you examine your personality? Because it is what you express in all areas of your life, including your work. We desire work that feels comfortable to us, where we can be ourselves, and where we can use our strengths. As you read through this chapter and complete the recommended exercises, think about how you may choose to express your personality in all areas of your life. Ideally, you will aspire to work in an environment that uses your best. When you are unable to integrate yourself in the work place, you will need to consider other areas for self expression, through your family life, hobbies or avocations. Careers develop over a life span and often change. Thus, you may have the opportunity to express different aspects of yourself as you grow and change. You are not stagnant and your life is not static. Allow your career to mature with your own metamorphosis.

Several personality theories and inventories apply to career exploration. Personality or interest inventories help categorize your interests and personal traits into classifications. Although no theory suggests that there is a limited number of personality types, they do suggest that we possess certain characteristics that are associated with particular types.

Often individuals, by stressing the importance of the categories, overlook the real information a personality assessment is offering. The primary goal of any self-assessment exercise or inventory is to help you understand yourself. It is not important to find a particular category in which you belong. Assessment results, personality types, and occupational clusters should be used as a tool in helping you recognize your personality characteristics, your values, what you like and don't like, or in other words, who you are. With this self-understanding you no longer need outside sources to tell you what you should be doing, or at what you might be good. In reading this chapter, keep in mind that you need to identify your characteristics, qualities and strengths and think about how they may parallel certain career paths.

A widely used theory, developed by John H. Holland (1973), suggests that individuals with similar interests and values tend to choose similar work environments. Individuals employed in work environments appropriate for their personalities will be satisfied with their jobs. Holland proposes six basic occupational environments and personalities. The six types of personalities are: **Realistic, Investigative, Artistic, Social, Enterprising,** and **Conventional.** The types form a matrix (see Figure 1), with those next to each other being more similar, and those across from each other least similar. Thus, the Conventional type is least like the Artistic type. The Realistic and Conventional types are more similar to each it with its neighbors: Realistic and Investigative personalities prefer to work with things. Investigative and Artistic types work with abstracts. Artistic and Social types are involved with feelings. The Social and Enterprising personalities are both leaders. The Enterprising and the Conventional types work on tasks. The Conventional and Realistic personalities prefer structured and methodical work. You will find you have some characteristics from all the six types. You may identify strongly with a particular personality. You may identify with just a few. Combine the top two or three Holland types to help identify which occupational environments you prefer. Table 4 provides descriptions, lists of abilities, college majors and general occupational fields for each of the types.

Often individuals score high in types that are adjacent to each other on Holland's matrix. If you receive high scores in areas opposite each other, such as Artistic and Conventional, Social and Realistic, or Enterprising and Investigative, it merely indicates that you have personality traits from very different types. It will be more difficult to find occupations that have opposite personality prerequisites. Some examples are: a Social-Realistic occupation is physical education teacher; an Enterprising-Investigative occupation is marketing researcher; and an Artistic-Conventional occupation is pottery maker. If you cannot find suitable occupations, you may have to express those aspects of your personality that do not fit into your career aspirations during your free time, or at another time in your life. Just remember it is important to recognize and express all of your personality.

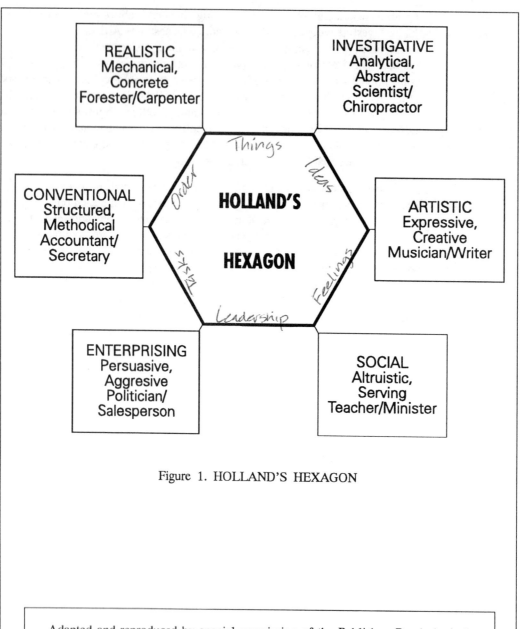

Figure 1. HOLLAND'S HEXAGON

TABLE 4 - HOLLAND'S PERSONALITY TYPES AND OCCUPATIONAL ENVIRONMENTS*

REALISTIC

PERSONALITY: Realistic types prefer relating to the physical world. They enjoy activities in which they work with tools, objects or animals, and avoid activities demanding social situations. They focus on the concrete. They are independent. They like working in systematic and explicit environments. They learn best through doing with their hands, not through formal schooling.

Descriptive Words: Strong minded, discipline, mechanical, conserving, materialistic, reserved, physical, concrete, straightforward, technical, matter-of-fact, steadfast, pragmatic.

ENVIRONMENT: The Realistic environment often is outdoors working with machines, tools, plants or animals. They like methodical, uniform and straightforward environments. Occupations may involve physical strength or agility, and/or mechanical knowledge.

College Major: Industrial Arts, Applied Sciences, Agriculture.

Abilities: Numerical, Manual Dexterity, Mechanical, Spacial.

Fields: Agriculture, Natural Resources, Vehicle/Machine Operation or Repair, Military, Law Enforcement, Construction, Skilled Crafts, Equipment Repair.

---

*Adapted and reproduced by special permission of Psychological Assessment Resources, Inc., Odessa, FL 33556, from the *Self-Directed Search Professional Manual* and *Manual Supplement* by John L. Holland, Ph.D. Copyright 1985 and 1987, respectively, by PAR, Inc. Further reproduction is prohibited without permission from PAR, Inc.

TABLE 4 - Continued

INVESTIGATIVE

PERSONALITY: The Investigative types like to observe, analyze and understand. They are intellectual. They are primarily concerned with the abstract and ideas. When they work with objects, the object is a tool for formulating an idea, e.g. chart, book, calculator. When they work with people, it is also from a distance, as in theorizing.

Descriptive Words: Analytical, conceptual, rational, discerning, introspective, intellectual, complex, cognitive, unassuming, abstract, contemplative, inquisitive, speculative.

ENVIRONMENT: The Investigative types choose environments in which they may engross themselves in a project. They desire independence from time and people constraints. Procedures will be their own. They utilize tools, such as, books, computers, calculators, lab equipment and maps.

College Major: Sciences, Social Sciences, Humanities.

Abilities: Reading, Numerical, Language Usage, Scientific.

Fields: Medical, Engineering, Natural or Physical Sciences, Mathematics, Social Sciences.

TABLE 4 - Continued

ARTISTIC

PERSONALITY: The Artistic types are creative, and may express themselves aesthetically, or in drama and literature. They like exploring the unknown. They desire freedom to work at their own pace and intensity, with few guidelines and rules to follow.

Descriptive Words: Ingenious, expressive, individualistic, inspirational, nonconformist, spontaneous, creative, imaginative, visionary, impulsive, intuitive, eccentric, sensitive.

ENVIRONMENT: Artistic environments must provide freedom to work at own pace and intensity with no guidelines or rules to follow. They prefer personally or aesthetically pleasing settings. Their tools are used to create, such as, typewriters, canvas and paints, or musical instruments.

College Major: Arts, Humanities, Communications.

Abilities: Language Usage, Spacial, Mental Creative, Creative Expression.

Fields: Applied Arts, Creative/Performing Arts, Languages, Advertising & Public Relations, Journalism, Liberal Arts.

TABLE 4 - Continued

SOCIAL

PERSONALITY: The Social types like to help, inform, guide and cure people. They are empathic and sensitive to others. They are at home with interpersonal relations. They enjoy helping, leading, nurturing or serving.

Descriptive Words: Nurturing, influential, perceptive, altruistic, collaborative, communicative, serving, merciful, empathetic, tolerant, benevolent, gracious.

ENVIRONMENT: The Social environment is people-oriented. They prefer active settings that include interacting, helping, teaching, and leading capacities.

College Major: Education, Social Science, Liberal Arts, Health Care.

Abilites: Language Usage, Reading, Leadership.

Fields: Health Care, Education, Social Service, Government Service, Religious Service, Communications.

TABLE 4 - Continued

ENTERPRISING

PERSONALITY: The Enterprisers like to manage and lead others to attain organizational goals or economic gains. They are persuasive and energetic. They may initiate something, but get others to carry out the task.

Descriptive Words: Persuasive, extrovert, poised, aspiring, bold, ambitious, energetic, authoritative, prestigious, vivacious, self-assured, extravagant, domineering.

ENVIRONMENT: The Enterprising environment is fast pace. If in an office setting, there must be no restrictions on coming and going. They prefer a prestigious, impressive looking environment with office/business tools.

College Major: Social Science, Business, Liberal Arts.

Abilities: Numerical, Language Usage, Sales, Leadership, Management, Organization.

Fields: Marketing, Sales, Record Management, Finance, Communication, Management.

TABLE 4 - Continued

CONVENTIONAL

PERSONALITY: The Conventional types like to carry out tasks in a systematic and orderly manner. They feel most comfortable with rules and regulations, and are uncomfortable with exploratory and ambiguous situations. They like working with data and procedure initiated by others.

Descriptive Words: Methodical, meticulous, conforming, economical, secular, efficient, prudent, punctual, careful, controlled, formal, earnest, orderly.

ENVIRONMENT: The Conventional environment is neat and orderly in an office setting often within a large company. Tools are typewriters, calculators, and other office machines, and handbooks. They desire secure jobs with regular hours.

College Major: Business, Liberal Arts.

Abilities: Numerical, Language Usage, Organization, Clerical.

Fields: Finance, Business Machines or Computer Operations, Clerical, Business Administration.

EXERCISE 4 A - THE REAL YOU

Think about a time and place in your life in which you felt totally comfortable with yourself. Return to a time when you were not playing any role and when you felt that you could express the real you. This may have been when you were very young. It may have been a certain period in your life. It may have been when you were around a certain person (who allowed you to be who you are). It may have been a certain situation or activity in which you were engrossed.

Clearly imagine that time and place. Use all your senses. Picture your surroundings. What does it look like? What are you wearing? What colors are present? What do you smell? What sounds do you hear? Who are you with? What are you doing? Imagine yourself completely comfortable and content at what you are doing.

When you are ready, conclude this memory and write a description of the environment, including what you did and who was there. List some adjectives that characterize you in this memory.

After completing the exercise look over Table 4 and see which personality type(s) best match the description of you. Summarize the real you on your Personal Exploration Summary.

EXERCISE 4B - FANTASY WORK ENVIRONMENT

Think about your fantasy place of employment. Describe the surroundings. Is it indoors, or outdoors? Are you in a sky scraper with a window office? Or do you even have an office? Do you travel? Do you work at home? Do you work with others? Do you work alone? Or both? What is your relationship with your co-workers? What kinds of tools or machines do you use? Is your environment fast or slow pace? What is your boss like?

Write down as much detail as you can imagine about your work environment. After you have completed this exercise look over Table 4 and see which environment(s) are closest to your description. Summarize your environment on your Personal Exploration Summary.

EXERCISE 5 - MANIFEST THE REAL YOU

Picture yourself in your current or a past job. Picture the work environment. List the characteristics from Exercise 4A and 4B (the real you) that you express at work. Answer the following questions:

1.   Which characteristics that are stifled at work would you like to express?

2.   How would you go about expressing these chracterics at work?

3.   How would you go about expressing these characteristics in other areas of your life?

SMITH FAMILY

4B - FANTASY WORK ENVIRONMENT

ANNE:

I'd like to work around old, but beautiful, things. I like the smell of old things, like when you're in a museum, or a large library. I want to be reminded of history. If I were to be in an office that was modern or ugly, I would bring in my own things. I'd also have to be around people, not constantly, but most of the time. I would like people to come to me for advice or information. I need to be active and make things happen.

MIKE:

I'd prefer to be outdoors. I always said, I'd like to install my computer on the patio and sit in the sun. The weather would have to be nice. Of course, if this is a fantasy, throw away the computer. I'd want to be in some meadow, or marsh watching birds or mammals. Adventure at my age? I would not need people around for days. Tools? Nothing backbreaking, at least not most of the time. How about a camera, and pencil and paper? A vehicle for getting around.

SEAN:

Definitely the skyscraper type of building- real modern. Lots of windows. I'd want to be able to move around, go to lunch, travel, not be stuck behind a desk. I want a nice office, though. I'd have a secretary. People are all coming to me because I'm in charge and make the decisions. They both love and respect me. After work we all go to a bar or something and hang out. It's real fast pace.

MARY:

An office all to myself where I won't be disturbed by anyone. I want to be able to be so absorbed in my work that nothing else matters. It needs to be something creative. I could work on something day and night and not know where the time is. I'd like to be able to work when I want to, like, I work best late at night. I'd don't need to be around people, but I'd like to be with people who are into the same thing I am, and we could be intensely involved in a project, but we work separately.

RESOURCES FOR ASSESSING PERSONALITY

ASSESSMENTS:

Myers-Briggs Type Indicator, Consulting Psychologist Press, P.O. Box 10096, Palo Alto, California 94303. (800) 624-1765*

Sixteen Personality Factor Questionnaire, by Raymond B. Carttell, Ph.D., D. SC. Institute for Personality and Ability Testing, Inc., P.O. Box 188, Champaign, IL 61824. (800) 225-4728*

Strong-Campbell Interest Inventory, Consulting Psychologist Press. P.O. Box 10096, Palo Alto, CA 94303. (800) 624-1765*

The Self-Directed Search, A Guide to Educational and Vocational Planning, by John L. Holland, Ph.D., Psychological Assessment Resources, Inc., P.O. Box 998, Odessa, FL 33556. (800) 331-TEST

BOOKS:

Life Types, by Sandra Hirsh and Jean Kummerow. Warner Books, New York, 1989.

Making Vocational Choices: A Theory of Vocational Personalities & Work Environments, by John L. Holland. Prentice Hall: Englewood Cliffs, 1985.

Please Understand Me, by David Kiersey and Marilyn Bates. Prometheus Nemesis Book Company, Box 2082, Del Mar, CA 92014. (619) 632-1575.

Gifts Differing, by Isabel Briggs Myers. Consulting Psychologist Press, Palo Alto, 1989.

*These personality assessments may be obtained from a career counselor or other licensed counselor.

CHAPTER IV:

VALUES

$\mathbf{W}$hat is a value? The dictionary says that a value is a principle, standard, or quality considered worthwhile or desirable. Values are your intrinsic and extrinsic motivators. Extrinsic values are based on an external gain, for instance, studying hard for a test to receive a good grade. This external gain may help you achieve your goal, as in graduating from college so you can get a good job. The extrinsic value is not in the college degree but what the degree can do for you. Intrinsic values are those that are a reward in themselves, for instance, studying for the satisfaction of learning. In this instance, learning or knowledge is the value. Your values not only encourage and enable you to attain your goals, they also determine your goals and the path you choose to achieve your goals. For instance, if you want material wealth, you will seek an occupation that has high earnings so you can buy things. The money you receive, in return, motivates you to work toward a promotion and a raise in your salary. If you choose industriousness to achieve this promotion, you will work hard to obtain your goal. On the other hand, if you value cunning, you will more likely use shrewd methods for getting that raise.

American culture, however, values youth. Consequently, we spend a great deal of effort and money to look, feel, and act young. Some Asian cultures emphasize family or group loyalty, whereas American culture values rugged individualism. These cultural values may diverge as the circumstances of our society alter. If our country was at war, our values would undergo a change. If we grew up in a depression our values would be different.

NEEDS AND VALUES

Values are also influenced by our needs. Abraham Maslow (1970), identified five basic needs that progress on a hierarchy, beginning with physiological/survival needs and ending with spiritual/philosophical needs. One moves to the next level on the hierarchy only after fulfilling the needs on the preceding level (See Figure 2). Our values are determined by the level at which our needs have been fulfilled.

If we are hungry and cold, we will value food and warmth. If we feel alone, we will value friendship. If we are ill, we will value health. In these situations of need we often value that which we do not have, or that which is difficult for us to acquire.

As our circumstances change, our values change. Take, for instance, a woman with children who lives comfortably and has a husband to help support the family financially. Her values will change if her husband dies, or if she divorces. She will need to provide for her family on her own. A secure job, money, a comfortable place to live become more important than a vacation abroad, or buying a new house. As this woman becomes more financially secure her values may change, again. She may consider returning to school so she can find a job that is more challenging. Or, she may consider a vacation, or moving to a nicer home.

A college student who is seeking independence from his parents will change his values after being financially independent and upon achieving basic career goals. While still living at home, independence is an important value. Upon achieving independence, financial security, challenge or recognition may become more important values. As you can see, several factors continue to influence our values. Culture, environment, family and individual needs can result in some unique combinations of who we are and what we want from life.

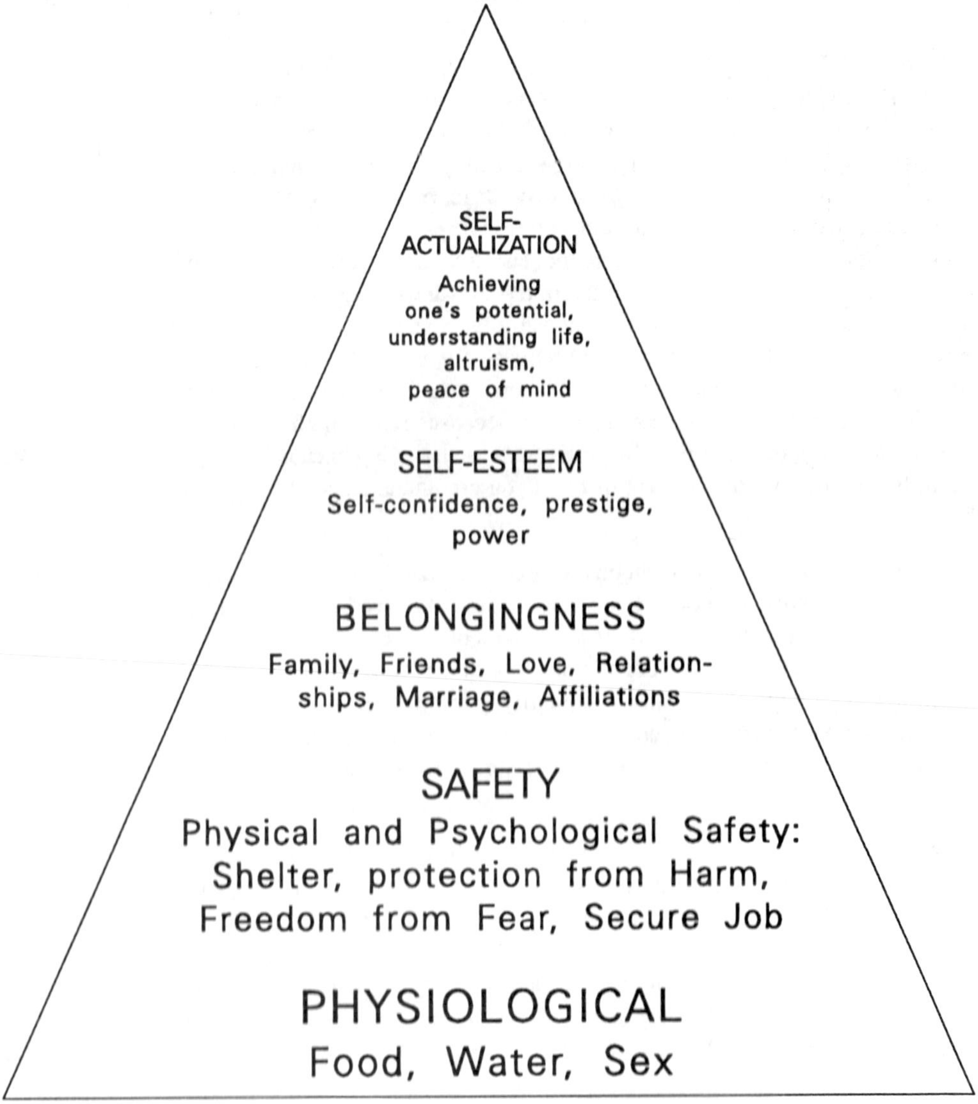
SELF-
ACTUALIZATION
Achieving
one's potential,
understanding life,
altruism,
peace of mind
SELF-ESTEEM
Self-confidence, prestige,
power
BELONGINGNESS
Family, Friends, Love, Relation-
ships, Marriage, Affiliations
SAFETY
Physical and Psychological Safety:
Shelter, protection from Harm,
Freedom from Fear, Secure Job
PHYSIOLOGICAL
Food, Water, Sex

Figure 2. ABRAHAM MASLOW'S HEIRARCHY OF NEEDS

WORK VALUES

Frederick Herzberg (1966) has examined job satisfaction among workers, and categorizes work motivation into two types: internal and external. These motivators are a result of our internal and external values. External motivators fall under Maslow's first three needs: physiological, safety and belongingness. Some external values from these needs are: economic returns, opportunity for advancement, work environment and relationships with supervisors and co-workers. Internal motivators match the last two needs on the hierarchy: self-esteem and self-actualization. Some internal values are: creativity, work in field of interest, achievement, recognition, responsibility. Sometimes we choose jobs because of the external values they fulfill. Unless our internal values are being satisfied somewhere else in our lives, we will soon tire of the job based on external values. For example, you may choose a job because of the high salary and opportunity to travel, but later find that you resent the traveling because you miss your family, and in spite of the great income, you are unchallenged by the work itself.

Since much of our time is spent on the job, we need to look at our values and how they fit in the world of work. If you value financial rewards, then it may not matter to you that you will need to work long hours on the job in order to receive those rewards. If you value knowledge, it may not matter to you that you need to spend ten years in college. If you value your family, you may turn down a promotion that will warrant a lot of traveling and prevent you from spending time at home. If you value independence, you may risk job security for the opportunity to be your own boss.

We are not always consciously aware of our values when deciding on a job. Even when we do ponder over these things, we sometimes feel impelled to go with secondary values because we are influenced by our cultural/societal values. Often we have several values that may produce conflicting results. Some typical middle class American values are financial security, family, independence and education. We may need to compromise between some of these values. So how do we choose? How do we know what we choose now will be important to us later? It becomes necessary for us to look at what is most important to us at this time in our life, and to realize that this may change as we get older and our circumstances alter.

We have some basic core values that stick with us throughout life. These are the values that are closely related to our personality as a whole. In this chapter we will make an effort to discover your core values.

EXERCISE 6 - WORK VALUES INVENTORY

Circle below how important the statements are to you.

1 = not at all important   **2 = not very important**
3 = somewhat important   **4 = very important**

It is important that...

1.	...through my work I add beauty to the world.	1	(2)	3	4
2.	...I continue to learn and understand new things.	1	2	3	(4)
3.	...I have status at work.	1	(2)	3	4
4.	...I have different tasks and responsibilities.	1	(2)	3	4
5.	...my work does not interfere with my personal life.	1	2	3	(4)
6.	...my work contributes to the welfare of society.	1	2	3	(4)
7.	...my job provides security.	1	2	(3)	4
8.	...I use my ideas to make new things.	1	(2)	3	4
9.	...I like the people with whom I work.	1	2	3	(4)
10.	...my job gives me standing in the community.	1	(2)	3	4
11.	...I have the opportunity to lead others.	(1)	2	3	4
12.	...I have the opportunity to choose my own work.	1	2	3	(4)
13.	...I am interested in the work I do.	1	2	3	(4)
14.	...my job permits me to live the kind of life I choose to live.	1	2	3	(4)
15	... I see the results of my work.	1	2	3	(4)

(Continued)

EXERCISE 6 - Continued

16.   ...my job pays well.   1 2 3 (4)

17.   ...I like the surroundings in which I work.   1 2 3 (4)

18.   ...I get along with my supervisor.   1 2 3 (4)

19.   ...I help others.   1 2 3 (4)

20.   ...I don't get bored at work.   1 2 3 (4)

21.   ...I work in a field that interests me.   1 2 3 (4)

22.   ...I work in surroundings that are beautiful.   1 2 (3) 4

23.   ...my work intellectually stimulates me.   1 2 3 (4)

24.   ...I plan and direct the work of others.   (1) 2 3 4

25.   ...I don't need to worry about being laid off or losing my job as long as I do it well.   1 2 3 (4)

26.   ...I use my creativity.   1 2 3 (4)

27.   ...I set my own hours.   1 2 3 (4)

28.   ...I have a respectable occupation.   1 2 3 (4)

29.   ...my job does not dominate my life style.   1 2 3 (4)

30.   ...I use my skills in my work.   1 2 3 (4)

31   ...I earn a great deal of money.   1 2 3 (4)

32.   ...I enjoy my co-workers.   1 2 3 (4)

33.   ...I create beautiful things.   1 2 (3) 4

34.   ...I can pursue my own ideas.   1 2 (3) 4

(Continued)

35.	...I have the opportunity to explore new ideas.	1	2	3	(4)
36.	...I manage others.	(1)	2	3	4
37.	...my work has variety.	1	2	(3)	4
38.	...my work allows me to develop my potential.	1	2	3	(4)
39.	...my work helps make the world a better place.	1	2	3	(4)
40.	...my work surroundings are pleasing to me.	1	2	3	(4)
41.	...I earn enough to be very comfortable.	1	2	3	(4)
42.	...I feel my work is worthwhile.	1	2	3	(4)
43.	...I work in surroundings that are comfortable.	1	2	3	(4)
44.	... I can stay with my job as long as I work hard.	1	2	3	(4)
45.	...I may be innovative at work.	1	2	(3)	4

(Continued)

EXERCISE 6 - KEY :
Add the amounts for each item number:

Instructions: The values with scores of nine or above are those you have indicated are important. Take all the values with scores nine or above and put them in rank order with number one as the work value most important to you, two the value second most important, and so on. You may not have any ties. List your five top work values on your Personal Exploration Summary.

Aesthetics - Opportunity to add beauty to the world.
To work in beautiful surroundings.

1, 2 22, 3 33 3   8

Independence - Choose one's own tasks, and work at one's own rate.

12, 4 27, 4 34 3   12

Intellectual stimulation - Independent thinking and continual learning.

2, 4 23, 3 35 4   11

Leadership - Opportunity to lead others at work.

11, 1 24, 1 36 1   3

Prestige - Work that brings about recognition and respect

3, 2 10, 2 28 4   8

Field of Interest - To work in field of interest, to use one's skills, and to continue to grow in field of training.

13, 4 21, 4 30 4   12

Variety - Job with different tasks and duties.

4, 2 20, 4 37 3   9

Way of Life - Job permits one to live the kind of life one chooses, with no restrictions in behavior and life style.

5, 4 14, 4 29 4   12

Achievement - Accomplishment; development of potential; see results of work.

15, 4 38, 4 42 4   12

Altruism - Work that enables one to contribute to the welfare of others.

6, 4 19, 4 39 4   12

Associates - Like coworkers and supervisors.
Frequent contact with fellow workers.

9, 4 18, 4 32 4   12

(Continued)

EXERCISE 6 - KEY - Continued

Creativity - To create or design new ideas or things. 8, 2 26, 4 45 3 9

+ Economic Returns - Job that pays a great deal. 16, 4 31, 4 41 4 12

Economic Security - Job that will be there during
hard times. 7, 3 25, 4 44 4 11

1 field of interest
2 way of life
3 altruism
4 independence
5 economic returns
6 associates
7 achievement
8 economic security

EXERCISE 7A - OWNING YOUR VALUES

Pick one of the suggestions below. Consider all aspects of the situation. Underline each item you feel is very important in your life. Answer these questions: Why are your values important to you? Are those values underlined *REALLY* yours? How do your values differ from your parents' values?

1. Make a list of things your immediate family valued.

2. Make a list of the values of your culture/religion/immediate society.

3. Ask your parents what was important to them when they were your age.

EXERCISE 7B - VALUES IDENTIFICATION

Pick one of the examples below. Think in detail and vividly describe each situation. Leave out shoulds, and assume you have no limitations. I do not want you to censor your values!

1. What is it that you most want from life *for you* (not anyone else)?

2. If you were to win the million dollar lottery, what would you do/buy?

3. If you could design your life from the beginning what would it be like?

4. If you had a whole week to yourself, what would you do? (Do not consider this as a vacation.)

5. If you could be anyone you like, what kind of person would that be?

6. If you were to give a gift of life to your child, what would you give that person (no limitations)?

7. Describe your perfect day.

8. Pretend that your life is over. What would you want people to remember about you?

9. Make a list of all the things you would like to accomplish in your life.

(Continued)

EXERCISE 7B - Continued

Analyze the results in three steps:

1. Check the values in **Table 5 - Personal Values** that appeared in your descriptions for **Exercises 7A - Owning Your Values,** and **7B - Values Identification.**

2. Prioritize the values.

3. Underline each value that is already satisfied in your life.

Keep your list for later use (Exercise 18 - Goal Setting). List your five top personal values on your Personal Exploration Summary.

TABLE 5 - PERSONAL VALUES CHECKLIST

✓ 1.   Family - Spending a great deal of time with family members.

✓ 2.   Marriage or love relationship - Desiring a fulfilling marriage or love relationship.

✓ 3.   Self-confidence - Belief in your own abilities, goals and desires.

✓ 4.   Faith - Loyalty to one's belief (may be religious or spiritual).

5.   Power - Having authority and/or influence over others.

✓ 6.   Financial Security - The assurance that you will always live comfortably.

✓ 7.   Altruism - Unselfish concern for the welfare of others.

✓ 8.   Health - To live a long and healthy life.

✓ 9.   Peace of Mind - Having emotional and spiritual well being.

✓ 10.   Aesthetics - Sensitive to beauty and harmony.

✓ 11.   Knowledge - Be well informed and continue to learn.

12.   Creativity - Bring about original and imaginative ideas or things.

13.   Equality - Equal opportunity for fellow human beings.

✓ 14.   Freedom - Free to do and think what you want and be who you want.

15.   Prestige - Reputation based on high achievement and character.

✓ 16.   Wisdom - Having good judgment, being informed.

17.   Tradition- Following a set of customs or behavior.

✓ 18.   Physical - Being physically fit and able to do physical things, (e.g., exercise, play sports).

COMPROMISING:

It was probably difficult for you to prioritize your values in Part 7B because you had to make a choice between some very strong desires. Understanding what is *MOST* important to you will help a great deal in making decisions and setting goals. If there is a conflict in your values, think of possibilities that will allow you to fulfill both ends of the conflict. You may not be able to fulfill everything in your job. You may not be able to fulfill all your values in your first job. You may fulfill some things at work, and other things in your leisure time. It may take several years of hard work in your field to achieve the recognition you value. You may not be able to fulfill all your needs to be creative in a job. Therefore, you may use your excess creativity with a hobby.

The idea is to fulfill all your values both in work and in your personal life, and not give up any values. They are part of who you are. You may forget about an unfulfilled value because you haven't thought about it for so long, and it has been buried deep inside of you. It isn't healthy to ignore any part of you.

When we are children, we frequently are told to not express things because it isn't polite, or because it is selfish, or because it may hurt someone's feelings. We need to learn to balance our own values with those of our mates and/or loved ones. Our task is, thus, to rediscover our values and to realize their importance. The creative part of values clarification is discovering how to fulfill all your values without too much compromising. It may be possible if you keep in mind that you have your whole life to fulfill who you are.

SMITH FAMILY

Exercise 6 - Work Values Inventory

Exercise 7A - Owning Your Values

Exercise 7B - Values Identification

MIKE

Exercise 6: 1) Independence; 2) Field of Interest; 3) Intellectual Stimulation; 4) Achievement; 5) Altruism.

Exercise 7A: Parents/societal values: <u>marriage/family</u>, <u>financial security</u>, <u>stability/responsibility</u>, <u>prestige</u>, <u>health</u>. I think because my parents grew up in the depression they are more concerned about security than I am. I think I am more concerned about the quality of life, most likely because we have more choices than our parents. I am also more concerned with aesthetics, and keeping our environment beautiful. Again, that is a more recent concern for our culture. All in all, my values closely match those of my parents.

Exercise 7B: Accomplish: Reviewing my life and I'm 95 years old. I would want to know that I had done the basic things a man is suppose to do: raise a family with kids, be an honest man, be successful (in my own terms), have a sense of humor. I'd like to leave behind more than my own biological creations. For instance, intensely study a particular animal, or write a book. I would like my discovery to reflect who I am. I would want it to make an impact on the world, change some of the wrongs. I don't want this for any fame it would give me, although I will admit I enjoy recognition. I would not want it to change my life. I'd want to live a normal life.

(Continued)

SMITH FAMILY - Continued

Values in rank order: <u>Marriage and family</u>, <u>self-confidence</u>, <u>knowledge</u>, freedom, altruism, prestige. The last three values are somewhat fulfilled, but not to the degree I would like. This is especially true in my work environment. I am unsure of how to resolve this without starting over in a new profession, one that closely matches my true interests and still have the financial security I have today.

SMITH FAMILY - Continued

ANNE:

Exercise 6: Aesthetics, Way of Life, Economic Security, Independence, Variety.

Exercise 7A. Parental/societal values: <u>Marriage/family</u>, being a good homemaker, <u>financial security</u>, unselfishness, prestige through husband, <u>education, industriousness.</u> The only conflict between my values and that of my parents generation is in the role of the wife/mother. I have lived pretty closely to my mother's values. I am no longer sure that it is something I would do again, or recommend for my daughter.

Exercise 7B. Typical Week: I'll start the week finishing off a trip to Europe with my husband. The trip is both business and pleasure. I am hitting auctions in several of the cities we vacation. On this occasion we are in London, I am at an auction during the day and in the evening we have dinner at an Indian restaurant, and then go to the theatre. The following morning we take a train into Oxford and spend the following two days bike riding and camping through the country side. We stay at a bed and breakfast. We ride our bike for several hours, then picnic. Mike will have his bird book and choose to scout around. I will read a book or visit historical sights. On the fourth day we return home. We live in a semi-rural area, a compromise between my husband, who likes the country, and me.

The drive to my antique shop in the city takes only 30 minutes. My husband works at a local university on a part time basis. He also works at home. I go into work every day for five hours. I have a business partner, and some help. My partner and I trade off traveling. We only sell very high quality pieces. I meet my partner at work and we discuss my trip and financial expenses. I don't worry about getting home, because I know my husband will take care of dinner. On the week end both my children visit for a day.

(Continued)

SMITH FAMILY - Continued

Values: Marriage and family, financial security, self-confidence, work I love, and travel. Doing this exercise makes me realize that I have a lot of what I want from life. The missing link is work I love, and with that I believe I'll gain self-confidence. I have self-confidence in my life right now, but am fearful of the world of work. The conflict in doing the work I love, I believe, also has to do with self-confidence. How does one gain self-confidence?

SMITH FAMILY - Continued

SEAN:

Exercise 6: Economic Returns, Leadership, Prestige, Achievement, Independence.

Exercise 7A. Parental values: <u>Financial security</u>, nature and beauty, knowledge, <u>self-confidence</u>, work and family. I am more into making money than my dad is. I'd like to be a corporate executive. My dad is a nature buff.

Exercise 7B. Lottery: I'd buy a house on the beach with servants and the works. I'd take a year off from school and travel all over the world first class. I'd buy a Ferrari. I'd hire someone to take care of my money so I would never have to work. I'd still want to work, just not have to work. I'd want houses or apartments in other places, but I could do that after all my traveling and after I've picked my favorite places. The only traveling we've done is the typical family kinds of trips to National Parks and once to Mexico, and Hawaii. After seeing the world and meeting the young jet set, I'd probably go back to school. I would just to do it to have something to fall back on, something to give me some background and experience. What I would really want is to start my own business. I'm not sure of what kind of business. I'd need to get some experience. I thought the prestigious school would help. I'd get my parents a house wherever they'd want.

Values: Financial security, freedom, prestige, power, <u>self-confidence</u>. I know I will have all my values fulfilled once I decide what I want to do with my life and education.

SMITH FAMILY - Continued

MARY:

Exercise 6: Creativity, Aesthetics, Way of Life, Independence, Intellectual Stimulation.

Exercise 7A. Parental values: <u>Marriage and family</u>, <u>freedom</u>, <u>education</u>, <u>aesthetics</u>, financial security, <u>health</u>. I think I'm more like my dad when it comes to values. Money and security doesn't mean that much to him. He does it for my mom. But I have her love for history and beautiful surroundings. I like nature too. Marriage and family are equally important as my career.

Exercise 7B. Design my life: To have grown up where everyone did something creative: a father who writes, a mother who paints. Someone would play music and we'd read to each other. Books everywhere. During summer vacations we'd travel to a summer house on a lake, or to Europe. It would be perfectly natural to write or paint, or play piano because I'd have done it all my life, and would not know any different. I'd go to an art school in a city like New York or Paris. All my friends are creative, and we'd stay up late at coffee houses talking about philosophy and literature. When I'm an adult I will travel all over the world and live in many places. I would not have to live anywhere in particular because I work at home. My husband would also be at home, and we would raise our children together, in the kind of environment I was raised. I don't aspire to be famous but would want to be respected for my work. I'd probably write novels, short stories or children's books. I'd like to work together with my husband. If I wrote children's books, he could illustrate them.

Values: <u>Creativity</u>, aesthetics, marriage, peace of mind, wisdom, freedom, and travel. I'm not sure that I will achieve all these things in my life as a writer. I am realistic enough to know that not all writers get published, and that it takes perseverance and hard work. I'm not sure I have what it takes, or the talent, for that matter.

CHAPTER V:

Interests

Interests are commonly used to help you determine your career options. Career inventories are frequently based on interests, and designed to have you choose your preferences from a variety of school subjects, careers, and leisure activities. Career information resources are categorized by interest clusters, such as the medical field, manufacturing, arts and entertainment. I will discuss more on the classification of career resources in Chapter IX, CAREER INFORMATION RESOURCES.

Your personality characteristics and values are closely related to your interests. Your interests are a simple way to define what you like and dislike at school and consequently in the world of work. You probably remember liking certain subjects at school when you were a kid, such as your social studies or art classes. And maybe you disliked math and gym. You may have preferred certain games to other games, some people to others, certain types of movies or books, or rock bands. This all tells a little about who you are. Of course, your interests change as you get older and as you experience different ideas and environments.

Exposure to wide variety of subjects, ideas, opportunities, styles, and so on, is important in selecting educational and career opportunities. Exposure and experimentation provide a basis for a healthy growing process. Whether you just completed high school, or are in midlife and changing your career, I encourage you to keep an open mind, and keep your opportunities optional until you have explored a great deal.

The most basic method of categorizing your interests is into DATA, PEOPLE, THINGS, and IDEAS.

DATA is anything from numbers, symbols and formulas, to words and maps. A lawyer needs data or information to defend a client, a writer needs data to express, an accountant records and computes data.

Those who work with **IDEAS** may use **DATA** or information to formulate a thought, a concept, a meaning or a plan. For instance, a scientist may have an idea for an hypothesis, a writer puts ideas into words, and a teacher assimilates and organizes ideas to present to students.

PEOPLE work is relating to people on all levels, including, taking orders and serving food, meeting together to complete a project, selling a product or service, or guiding others toward career goals.

Most jobs have some type of tool you may use, such as an alphabetizer, a bulldozer, a computer, pencil and eraser, paints, or screwdriver. When you prefer working with **THINGS**, the tool or machine is the basis of your work. For instance, a typist may not mind sitting behind a computer terminal all day, whereas a receptionist, who may also type, may prefer to answer phones and greet people because it provides the opportunity to be around people.

In Exercise 9 - Experience List, in the following chapter, you will categorize previous activities and accomplishments into data, people, things and ideas.

EXERCISE 8 - DATA/PEOPLE/THINGS/IDEAS

Going back to your Exercise 4 - Fantasy Work Environment, would you say that your ideal work environment was primarily data, people, things or ideas? If you are unsure, you may label each description in your environment as Data, People, Things and Ideas. Often people will find a combination of all four and will find it difficult to choose between all four. However, suppose you had to choose a job which only dealt with machines and/or tools, only worked with processing information, only required the use of ideas or only had to do with speaking to or signalling people. Which would it be? What is your second choice?

CHAPTER VI:

SKILLS

SKILLS ASSESSMENT

Assessing your skills is probably the most complex part of the career exploration process. Part of the difficulty is in our fear of not being good enough, and fear of failure. Inadequacy creates doubt and may decrease our interest in pursuing our dreams. We, however, tend to forget that skills can be learned. The second hurdle of skills analysis is identifying what our skills are. We often fail to make the connection between a career and the skills we have acquired from our varied experiences. We don't consider our day-to-day activity as skills. Suppose you are good at explaining homework assignments to your classmate. Or, suppose you can successfully arrange a dinner party at the last minute. Since you may do this type of thing all the time, you don't call it a skill. Because it is not something you do at your job, you don't consider it a skill.

Students often take my class to discover "what they are good at." I would not recommend choosing a career based on skills alone, for two reasons: you may be good at things you don't like doing, and you can learn the skills in which you are not yet proficient. It is important to consider both your interests as well as your skills. For example, you may be very good at cleaning your house, but does that mean you should be a housecleaner? You also want to determine whether you have the skills necessary for your career goal. But do not allow lack of ability to discourage you from achieving your goal. Because you were told that you were not good at math does not mean you can't acquire that skill.

It would be convenient to possess all the skills necessary for your chosen profession already. We all know individuals who excel in sports, have the knack for making their own clothes, have instant rapport with children or can fix anything in their house that is broken. These types of skills, which seem to come naturally, I call "talent." But even talented people need to work at their skills. There are Japanese craftsmen and artisans who, after working with their masters for over fifty years, are still considered apprentices.

To develop skills we need opportunity and nurturing. If you were raised in the type of environment where good study skills were encouraged, and where books were readily accessible, you had an advantage over someone whose environment lacked these things.

Measuring your skills as the only indicator for what you should be doing is unfair to you, and to the world. For instance, Anne had been interested in architecture as a child. When she discovered that she would need strong math skills, she did not pursue her childhood fantasy. Her parents and teachers did not encourage her ambitions because girls do not typically become architects. Anne did receive good grades in high school and attended college. Her best subject was history, and thus she considered teaching history. Had someone acknowledged Anne's interest in architecture and provided her with the opportunity to explore the field and meet an architect to ask questions or watch what he did on the job, it may have motivated her to do better in math, and to explore the field in more depth. Or, she may have found related areas in the field, and pursued one of them.

Assessing your skills includes: 1) discovering your abilities and aptitudes, 2) finding the skills necessary for your field of interest, and 3) determining the difference between the two. After you have established what occupation you want to pursue, you will identify the necessary skills, and determine which skills you already have and those you will need to learn. Once you know which skills you lack you can make plans to acquire them. As part of this process, you will consider the time and effort involved in learning these skills, and whether or not you are willing or able to pursue mastering them. Remember, not everyone starts at the same level.

SKILL CATEGFORIES

Skills are categorized into three types: personal, technical and functional/transferable.

PERSONAL (TRAITS): Your personal skills are your qualities, traits and characteristics. You emphasize all these personal qualities during an interview as you are convincing the interviewer that you are the right person for the job. Some examples of such qualities are: honesty, patience and caring.

TECHNICAL: Skills pertinent to a particular job or job cluster are technical. Some types of technical skills are: legal terminology, drafting, computer operation, understanding counseling theories and techniques, and flipping hamburgers. As you can see, these skills are acquired, either from special courses at school or previous work and life experiences. Sometimes these skills come easily, but usually some practice is required. Certain technical skills are used in a wide variety of job categories. Typing, for instance, is used in clerical positions, as well as in writing and computer programming. Knowledge of street language may be used by an undercover detective and also by a drug abuse counselor.

FUNCTIONAL: The last category of skills is called functional or transferable; they are skills that can be transferred from one job to another. Although personal qualities and technical skills can also be transferred, functional skills are the foundation necessary for a wide range of jobs. For instance, teachers write lesson plans, department managers write reports, and in many jobs one writes letters or memos. Waitresses organize their tables and orders to make the dining process flow smoothly. Supervisors organize work schedules or their subordinates' activities. Other examples of transferable skills are: coordinating, communicating, referring and directing.

Often young students think they don't have skills because they have never worked. Reentry homemakers don't believe they have job-related skills because they haven't worked outside the home in several years. Career changers may feel they do not have appropriate skills for the jobs they are seeking because they have not worked in those fields.

The purpose of the next assignment is to help you identify your skills from past experiences, whether they be actual jobs or other activities in your life. The result will include a list of skills you can use in various jobs or job functions.

EXERCISE 9 - EXPERIENCE LIST

An informal method of identifying your skills is by writing down your experiences and accomplishments. Consider activities from all areas in your life. Include: classes, extra-curricular activities, volunteer work, previous and current employment, special knowledge from hobbies, housework, and so on.

Step 1. List five of your best experiences or accomplishments. Pretend these experiences were jobs and write a detailed description of the job duties.

Step 2. Decide which of the specific duties or activities from these experiences you like, and which you would prefer not to do again. Next to those activities you like, put a plus sign. Put a minus sign next to those activities you dislike.

Step 3. Determine which specific action or activity involves data, people, things or ideas. Remember, some activities will include both or all interests.

Step 4. Count the total number of data, people, things, or ideas you signified for each specific activity you did enjoy performing (those with a plus sign). Put your preference of data, people, things or ideas on your Personal Exploration Summary in CHAPTER VIII - INTEGRATION.

EXERCISE 10 - SKILL CATEGORIES

Organize your skills (yes, these past experiences are your skills) into personal, technical and functional categories. Underline your functional and technical skills. If you cannot find the personal skill for an action or activity, use an adjective to describe what type of person would be able to perform that function. For instance, tutoring disabled students takes patience. Indicate your personal skills by putting parenthesis around the skill word. List your five best skills for each category on your Personal Assessment Summary.

Note: Keep your skill categories for Exercise 19 - Resume Preparation in CHAPTER XII DYNAMICS OF JOB SEARCH.

EXERCIZE 11 - INTEREST/SKILL INVENTORY

Circle those skills that you like or would like to use in a job. Assume that you are competent at all these skills.

1. Mechanical - Assemble, repair, or operate engines or machinery.

2. Make images - Draw, sketch, illustrate, paint, photograph.

3. Brainstorm - Think of new ideas.

4. Edit - Prepare written material suitable for publication or presentation.

5. Build or Construct - Make buildings, cabinets, clothing or other goods.

6. Organize - Pull together and arrange in order to develop projects.

7. Synthesize - Integrate ideas and information into a new whole idea.

8. Drive - Drive vehicle or machine.

9. Hypothesize - Propose a reason or theory that accounts for a set of facts which can be used as a basis for further investigation.

10. Design - Conceive, create or form plan for projects, programs or products.

11. Forecast - Estimate or calculate in advance.

12. Use intuition - Use insight, hunches and foresight.

13. Negotiate - Bargain for rights or advantages.

14. Act As Liaison - Serve as a link between individuals or groups.

15. Use Body Coordination - Use body strength, stamina and agility.

16. Initiate - Exert influence for bringing about new directions.

17. Budget - Plan for expenditure of money or resources.

18. Deal With Feelings - Listen, accept, empathize, calm and appreciate.

19. Classify - Categorize and systemize data or objects into classifications.

(Continued)

EXERCISE 11 - INTEREST/SKILL
INVENTORY - Continued

20. Teach - Inform, explain, give instruction or demonstrate.

21. Create - Originate, produce, or bring into being.

22. Supervise - Oversee and direct the work of others.

23. Read For Information - Thoroughly research written resources.

24. Perform - Express in artistic or entertaining form by singing, dancing, acting, playing music or speaking to an audience.

25. Counsel - Listen with objectivity; coach and encourage personal growth.

26. Install - Set in position and connect or adjust for use.

27. Analyze - Separate into parts or principals to examine nature of the whole.

28. Calculate/Compute - Use basic mathematics to compute quantities.

29. Work With Animals - Feed, shelter, breed, train or show pets or ranch animals.

30. Innovate - Begin or introduce something new.

31. Mediate - Resolve or settle conflicts or differences by acting as an intermediary.

32. Question - Caste doubt upon; search out.

33. Promote - Attempt to sell or popularize through the media or special events.

34. Write - Compose written forms of communication as in letters, articles, ads, stories, or lyrics.

35. Sell - Promote a person, company goods or services by convincing of merits.

36. Draft - Draw up plan based on specific dimensions or specifications.

(Continued)

EXERCISE 11 - INTEREST/SKILL
INVENTORY - Continued

37. Provide Hospitality - Welcome, provide pleasure to visitors, guests or customers.

38. Collaborate - Work together in joint effort.

39. Cultivate Plants - Grow food, flowers, trees or lawns.

40. Conceptualize - Form ideas or theories.

41. Visualize - Form a mental image of ideas or possibilities.

42. Maintain Records - Log, record, itemize, collate and tabulate data.

43. Technical - Use a specialized skill in scientific, industrial or other skilled field.

44. Invent - Originate a new idea or product through experimentation.

45. Navigate - Plan, record, control course of ship or aircraft.

46. Treat - Heal and take care of patients or clients.

47. Motivate - Stimulate, provide incentive, incite.

48. Use Dexterity - Skillful use of hands.

49. Research - Scholarly or scientific investigation.

50. Repair - Restore to original condition.

51. Problem Solving - Identify sources of a problem and provide a solution.

52. Delegate - Authorize others to take on tasks, assignments or workload.

53. Audit - Examine records for accuracy.

54. Work Outdoors - Work with nature and the environment. Spend most of your time outdoors.

(Continued)

EXERCISE 11 - INTEREST/SKILL
INVENTORY - Continued

55.   Compile - Gather facts or material.

56.   Operate Machinery - Use large or small machines to complete a task.

57.   Public Speaking - Present one's point of view to an audience with intent to inform.

58.   Assemble - Fit or join together parts.

TOTAL

DATA: 4 6 7 9 11 17 19 23 27 28 32 36 42 43 49 51 53 55

PEOPLE: 13 14 16 18 20 22 25 31 33 35 37 38 46 47 52 57

THINGS: 1 5 8 15 26 29 36 39 43 45 48 50 54 56 58

IDEAS: 2 3 7 9 10 12 21 24 27 30 32 34 40 41 44 51

NOTE: TABLE 7 - ORGANIZATION OF SKILLS arranges the above skills into data, people, things and ideas. Because these classifications are general, I have subcategorized them into the following: DATA - information management, information reasoning; PEOPLE - helping, leading, persuading; THINGS - general, specific; and IDEAS - creative, cognitive. Overlap between categories may exist. However, each category has a specific theme. For instance, not all individuals who like to work with people want to for the same reasons. Some may prefer to serve in a helping role, while others choose to lead or direct, and still others want to influence and persuade. People working with data may prefer record keeping tasks or use data to reason in scientific capacities, or in finance or business. Other individuals in scientific and scholarly environments may use data and ideas for cognitive reasoning. Others prefer ideas for creative pursuits. Those individuals working with things are usually in fields that require specific skills, and /or physical strength and agility.

TABLE 7 - ORGANIZATION OF SKILLS

DATA

Business Operation, Computer Operation, Academic & Scientific Research

INFORMATION MANAGEMENT

edit (4)
organize (6)
budget (17)
classify (19)
calculate/compute (28)
draft (36)
maintain records (42)
technical (43)
audit (53)

REASONING

synthesize (7)
hypothesize (9)
forecast (11)
read for information (23)
analyze (27)
question (32)
research (49)
problem solving (51)
compile (55)

PEOPLE

Social Service, Education, Religious Service, Health, Law & Politics, Sales & Marketing, Business Management, Hospitality

HELP

act as liaison (14)
deal with feelings (18)
teach (20)
counsel (25)
provide hospitality (37)
collaborate (38)
treat (46)
motivate (47)

LEAD

act as liaison (14)
initiate (16)
teach (20)
supervise (22)
mediate (31)
motivate (47)
delegate (52)
public speaking (57)

PERSUADE

negotiate (13)
initiate (16)
teach (20)
mediate (31)
promote (33)
sell (35)
motivate (47)
public speaking (57)

(Continued)

TABLE 7 - ORGANIZATION OF SKILLS

THINGS

Agriculture, Building Trades, Mechanical & Technological, Environmental

SPECIFIC

build/construct (5)
drive (8)
install (26)
draft (36)
cultivate plants (39)
navigate (45)
repair (50)
assemble (58)

GENERAL

mechanical (1)
use body coordination (15)
work with animals (29)
technical (43)
use dexterity (48)
work outdoors (54)
operate machinery (56)

IDEAS

Arts, Entertainment, Communications, Medicine, Engineering, Social
Physical and Natural Sciences

CREATIVE

make images (2)
brainstorm (3)
design (10)
use intuition (12)
create (21)
perform (24)
innovate (30)
write (34)
invent (44)

COGNITIVE

synthesize (7)
hypothesize (9)
analyze (27)
question (32)
write (34)
conceptualize (40)
problem solve (51)
visualize (41)

Exercise 9 - Experience List
Exerise l0 - Skill Categories

	LIKE DISLIKE	DATA PEOPLE THINGS IDEAS	TECHNICAL FUNCTIONAL

SEAN:
ACTIVITY

Student Body Representative:

convince school administration
to hire certain band (persuasive) ... + ... D,P,T ... F

plan and organize dances
(organized) ... + ... D,P,I ... F

find and hire bands
(assertive, negotiate) ... + ... D,P,T ... F

Electronics Shop:

intricate *knowledge* of stereo,
compact disc, speakers, cassette
players, etc. ... + ... D ... T

approach customers
(interpersonal) ... + ... P ... F

analyze customer type
(interpersonal, people savvy) ... + ... P ... F

influence decision-making
(persuasive) ... + ... P,D,I ... F

do inventory ... - ... D,T ... F,T

run computerized cash register ... + ... D,T ... F,T

handle cash, checks and
credit cards ... + ... D,T ... F,T

place orders ... + ... D ... F,T

handle exchanges and customer
problems (helpful, cool-headed) ... + ... P,D ... F,T

(Continued)

SMITH FAMILY - Continued

	LIKE DISLIKE	DATA PEOPLE THINGS IDEAS	TECHNICAL FUNCTIONAL
Sports:			
knowledge of rules and strategies	+	D,I	T
physical coordination and agility	+	T	T
lead and motivate others (leadership)	+	P	F
first aid and C.P.R.	+	D,P,T	T,F

DATA = 11. I enjoy using words to converse with people.

PEOPLE = 9. This does not reflect my true interest.

THINGS = 4. I don't mind using tools when they help get the job done.

IDEAS = 5. I would like to use ideas in a more advanced position.

    Personal Qualities: Independent, persuasive, friendly, extroverted, organized, verbal, opinionated, cooperative, leadership.

    Technical: Extensive stereo and electronics knowledge, salesmanship, first aid, baseball and soccer rules and strategy, physical agility and speed, C.P.R., basic computer: some programming in BASIC.

    Functional: Organize schedules and people, plan and organize events, verbal communication, as in persuading people to my point of view; can also explain basic ideas well, people-savvy — can easily identify peoples' interests and points of view.

MARY:	LIKE DISLIKE	DATA PEOPLE THINGS IDEAS	TECHNICAL FUNCTIONAL

ACTIVITY

Creative Writing Class:

Think up and write stories (creative)	+	I,D	F
Review movies: *analyze* plots and character motivation (analytical)	+	I,D	F
Analyze and critique books and stories	+	D,I	F
Edit other students' work (tactful)	+	D,P,I	T,F

Boutique Job:

Talk with customers	+	P	F
Ascertain needs (perceptive)	+	P,D	F
Find sizes or styles	+	D	F,T
Ring up cash register	-	D,T	F,T
Collect cash, checks, credit cards	-	D,T	F,T
Handle return items (patient)	-	D,P,T	F,T
Help customers decide (personable)	-	P	F
Count money (precise)	+	D	F,T

School Newspaper:

Research topics (reflective, thorough)	+	D,I	F
Interview people	+	P,D,I	F
Write stories (creative)	+	I,D	F
Layout and paste up of paper (detailed)	+	I,T,D	F
Edit and review work	+	D,I	F,T
Operate computer	+	T,D	T,F

(Continued)

SMITH FAMILY - Continued

DATA = 13. I like information, books, globes.

PEOPLE = 4. I like working with people in a cooperative situation. I don't like conflicts and I don't like selling. My people score would be higher if I had examples of doing pleasant things for and with people.

IDEAS = 8. I prefer ideas, thoughts, fantasies, but haven't had much opportunity except in writing or school subjects. I prefer the imaginary creative end of ideas.

Personal: Analytical, imaginative, reflective, intelligent, motivated, sensitive, thorough, tactful, idealistic.

Technical: Cash register, type letters, stories and papers (50 wpm), cook Italian, French and Thai food, write effective paper, knowledge of how newspaper works, knowledge of fashion trends, effective grammar usage.

Functional: Writing papers and stories, plan and organize papers and stories, plan and organize leisure, work and school schedules, analyze material read and researched, research topics of interest, creative in written expression.

MIKE:

ACTIVITY	LIKE DISLIKE	DATA PEOPLE THINGS IDEAS	TECHNICAL FUNCTIONAL
City Planner:			
Supervision:			
organize, coordinate and *supervise* work of unit planning activity (organized)	+	P,D,I	F
assign, review, evaluate and *redirect* work of subordinates	-	P,D,I	F
edit and combine work (methodical) of group into general report (precise)	+	D,I	F,T
present plans to agency staff and governing bodies	-	D,P,I	F
Research:			
Lay ground work in new programs	+	I,D	F,T
coordinate development of planning activity with other governmental groups	-	P,I	F,T
represent the city in meetings	-	P	F
Writing:			
generate reports from research findings	+	I,D	F,T
make analysis of findings in studies	+	I,D	F,T
make field observations	+	D,T,I	T,F
make regulations to planning projects (analytical)	+	D,I	F,T

Continued)

SMITH FAMILY - Continued

	LIKE DISLIKE	DATA PEOPLE THINGS IDEAS	TECHNICAL FUNCTIONAL
Handy Man:			
Basic *carpentry*	+	T,D	T
electrical	+	T	T
plumbing	-	T	T
masonry	+	T,D	T
auto mechanics	-	T	T
Biology/Zoology:			
knowledge and observation of animal habitat, survival, habits	+	D,T,I	T
Emphasis on birds, fresh water fishing	+	D,T,I	T
Basic Survival:			
Able to *survive* in wilderness	+	D,T	T,F
first aid	+	D,T	T
C.P.R.	+	D,T	

PEOPLE = 1. I am not convinced that I don't enjoy working with people as much as that I am constantly supervising people, as well as working with the public. A large part of my job is managing, and meeting with government and local agencies. I would like less people interaction, but certainly some; maybe on a more cooperative level.

DATA = 14. I enjoy gathering, analyzing and processing data.

THINGS = 9. I don't work with many things at my job, other than using the computer for some analysis. I noticed that my THINGS come from leisure activities. I would like to work more "in the field" so to speak and use tools, make things, etc.

IDEAS = 9. I like to work with ideas as a means to a solution or end.

(Continued)

SMITH FAMILY - Continued

Technical: Knowledge of: principles and methods of regional, county and city planning; legal implications of planning and zoning activity; research methods, statistics, computer programming (Fortran), birds, wilderness survival, fresh water fishing techniques.

Personal Qualities: Methodical, persistent, thorough, analytical, precise, critical, introspective, practical, resourceful.

Functional: Supervision, organization of groups and tasks, coordination of groups and tasks, public speaking, technical report writing, research, analysis, diplomatic contact with other agencies.

(Continued)

SMITH FAMILY - Continued

ANNE:

ACTIVITY

	LIKE DISLIKE	DATA PEOPLE THINGS IDEAS	TECHNICAL FUNCTIONAL
Christmas Bazaar			
Fund-raising:			
decide on what to sell (decisive)	+	I,D	F
make list of materials needed (organized)	+	D	F
find places that will donate or offer major discounts (resourceful)	+	I,D,P	F
organize and direct committees to help	+	I,D,P	F
find people to make or teach crafts	+	P,I,D	F
type mailing list	-	D,T	T,F
send invitations	-	D,T	F
make displays (creative)	+	T	T,F
decide on and *organize* activities	+	P,I,D	F
organize staff and kids	+	I,P	F
collect and count money (precise)	-	D,T	F,T
Furniture restoration:			
make contacts	+	P,D	F
learn about furniture periods and styles	+	D,I	F,T
know wood refinishing techniques	+	D,T	T
know where to buy materials	+	D	T
know how to refinish properly in order to keep authenticity	+	D,T	T
attend flea markets and auctions	+	P	F
sell (persuasive)	+	P,D,I	F
buy	+	P,D	F,T
price	+	D	F,T
Running Home:			
inventory and *budget* of household	+	D,T	F
keep house clean	-	T	F,T
delegate responsibility (responsible)	-	P	F

(Continued)

SMITH FAMILY - Continued

	LIKE DISLIKE	DATA PEOPLE THINGS IDEAS	TECHNICAL FUNCTIONAL
child care (discipline, nurture, listen, encouraging, motivating, patience!)	+	P,D,I	F,T
cooking and *planning* menus	+	D,I	F,T
planning parties, dinners, festive occasions	+	D,P,I	F
sewing and *mending*	-	T	T
decorate home (creative)	+	I,D,T,P	T,F
planning landscaping	+	I,D	T
gardening	-	T	T
nursing	+	P	T
knowledge of child development	+	I,D,P	T

DATA = 21. I am surprised how often data came up in my activities. I always thought of data in the context of statistics and to be very impersonal. Data or information which has to do with people interests me. I do enjoy finding out information to plan or accomplish what I need done.

THINGS = 6. This is accurate. I can use tools and equipment when necessary, but it is not a preference.

PEOPLE = 13. I believe my preference is to work with people. I have always enjoyed it most in all my activities. The higher score in data usually equates to an activity working with people. I plan to pursue a job with more people interaction.

IDEAS = 15. I like ideas, especially using my own.

Technical: Knowledge of child care/development, knowledge of furniture history, European historic events, knowledge of furniture refinishing techniques, ability to handle special tools, real estate knowledge from courses, budgeting/bookkeeping, typing, basic nutrition and menu planning, plant knowledge/landscaping/ horticulture.

Personal Qualities: Patient, organized, creative, nurturing, conscientious, cheerful, learn quickly, resourceful, adaptable, understanding, punctual, motivated.

Functional: Making contacts, organize, budget, plan, guide/teach, coordinate, delegate, research, make decisions, carry out imagined plan.

PART TWO

MAJOR AND
CAREER EXPLORATION

CHAPTER VII:

KNOW YOUR SCHOOL

Acquiring an education is more than taking courses, writing papers, sitting for exams, and receiving credits. Institutions of higher education offer a variety of resources, services and activities to enhance your educational experience. Awareness of the opportunities available, and understanding the basic steps towards graduation are important for your success at college. In this chapter I will review what types of educational resources are available to you. I will also discuss basic educational philosophies and current trends in higher education.

ENROLLMENT STATISTICS

Currently there are 3,400 institutions of higher education in the United States, enrolling 12.5 million students. Regardless of the drop in traditional students aged eighteen to twenty-four, there was an increase of 100,000 students between the 1986-87 and 1987-88 academic years.

Full time and part time enrollments are 7.2 million and 5.3 million respectively. Women outnumber men by 6.67 million to 5.88 million.*

Schools are generally categorized by the degrees they offer. In 1979, there were 1193 institutions that offered two-year degrees; 1471 offering bachelor's or master's degrees; and 427 doctoral programs. Approximately half of our institutions are under control of the federal, state and local government and encompass seventy-eight percent of the student body. The breakdown of college institutions falls into six major categories: 1) doctorate granting, 2) comprehensive universities and colleges, 3) liberal arts colleges, 4) two-year colleges or institutions, 5) professional schools or other specialized institutions, and 6) institutions for non-traditional study. Within these institutions, there are generally three types of education available to adults: vocational training, remedial and/or high school education, and college education.

There are state or public institutions, and private institutions. There are colleges and there are universities. Colleges grant bachelor degrees in liberal arts and in sciences. Universities have research and teaching facilities comprised of graduate and professional schools that award masters' degrees and doctorates, as well as undergraduate degrees, or bachelors' degrees. Institutions emphasizing teaching offer majors in fields that you can enter with only a bachelor's degree, such as, nursing, engineering or business. Research institutions tend to focus on the theoretical and research skills, and are best suited for students who intend to continue their education in graduate or professional programs. Universities will also differ in the degrees they offer. For instance, in California we have two state university systems: the California State University and the University of California. The first offers degrees to the masters' level. The second is considered a research institution and offers degrees to the doctorate level.

---

*National Education Association, Higher Education Advocate, Feb. 1988

TRENDS

In recent years, the average age of the college student has risen. In 1979, thirty-nine percent of college enrollment was the traditional college-age population of eighteen to twenty-four years old. A more recent survey by the College Board shows that six million adult students study for college credit every year. The board found that forty-five percent of all undergraduate students are over twenty-five years old and predicted an increase to fifty percent within a decade. Sixty percent of the over twenty-five adult population are women.*

Adults are returning to school for college degrees as well as special training such as computer literacy, business writing, high school subjects, or English as a second language. High school adult education is offered through local school districts at adult education centers, at high school campuses and at community colleges.

Two-year colleges offer vocational training, and a general college curriculum providing transfer opportunities to four-year universities and colleges. Private vocational schools frequently specialize in training in particular fields, such as business, travel industry or medical fields. The advantage of these schools is that their programs are accelerated and tailored for the working adult by offering courses at night and on weekends.

COMMUNITY COLLEGE

Community colleges, previously called junior colleges, have expanded and changed their roles over the years. During the seventies, "life- long learning for all" became the philosophy of the community college. Currently, forty-five percent of community college enrollment is over age 22. Twenty percent are first time college enrollees. Thirty-nine percent of all college minority students attend community colleges. With this change in the student body, the new two-year college is much more comprehensive than was the traditional junior college. It is committed to universal access, open-door admission, low tuition, local community orientation, program diversity and lifelong learning.

---

* M. W. Hirschorn, "Students over 25 Found to Make Up 45 Pct. of Campus Enrolments," *The Chronicle of Higher Education*, Mar. 30, 1988, p. A35

The basic types of curriculum provided are:

1. Courses that prepare one for particular employment in a defined job cluster, such as technology, business, medicine, and clerical. Community college vocational certificates are similar to those you would receive from a private vocational school. The certificate is different from the degree in that a degree would include general education requirements.

2. Associate of Arts and Associate of Science degrees may prepare you to transfer to the junior level of a baccalaureate degree program at a four- year college or university. Associate degrees are two year college degrees which include a major, as well as courses in general education. General education courses are designed to make you well rounded. At some community colleges, the A.S. and A.A. degrees do not prepare you to transfer to a four year institution but show basic preparation in a major field of study. In order to transfer to the four-year institution, you would follow specific guidelines outlined for transfer students.

3. Single courses or a cluster of courses designed to upgrade individual skills, or create new competence, as in computer, data entry or word processing training.

4. Courses that provide remedial, corrective and improvement education for those who have not previously mastered basic skills in literacy, mathematics or other basic subjects, including English as a second language.

5. Courses designed to upgrade individual skills, or create new competence as in computer or word processing training.

6. Courses to provide specific needs of people with learning impairments.*

The community college curriculum is closely tied into particular service organizations on campus. For instance, courses may be offered to students with learning disabilities through a Learning Disability Center. Community colleges are subsidized by the state and cost less than private colleges. Entry requirement is a high school diploma or being eighteen years old. Students who do not meet the requirements to attend four-year institutions frequently attend the two-year college. They may make up their high school course or grade deficiencies while preparing to transfer to the four-year college.

You *DO NOT* need an associate degree to transfer to a four year college or university. You need under-division courses equivalent to those required by the four-year institutions.

---

* Harold E. Mitzel (ed.), *Encyclopedia of Educational Research,* Vol. 2, 5th Ed. New York : The Free Press, 1982.

Associate degrees are designed for those students who do not expect to continue their education at a four-year institution yet should receive recognition for their educational endeavors. The two types of associate degrees are: Associate of Art (A.A.) and Associate of Science (A.S.). The distinction between the two is in the majors. A.A. degrees are awarded in fields such as the arts, humanities, social sciences, and languages. A.S. degrees are awarded in physical and biological sciences, engineering, business, and applied science and technology. A certificate program includes only the courses in a specialized field.

If you are unsure of how long you plan to attend college, and want to further your education, you have three options: to obtain a vocational certificate, to obtain an associate's degree, or to transfer to a four year institution. You may obtain your associate's degree and transfer as long as you have fulfilled the requirements for both of these options. Be sure that your college of entrance accepts your current major, and that you have completed the general education required for transferring to that particular institution.

Whenever you are intending to pursue any type of degree or certificate, see a college academic counselor. She can guide you toward the degree and courses appropriate for you. She knows which courses are transferable (which will count towards other colleges), what is necessary for your general education, and any policies and procedures of your college. Your college catalog also provides all of this information. I strongly recommend that you purchase your college's catalog.

STANDARD GRADUATION REQUIREMENTS AT THE COMMUNITY COLLEGE

The basic requirements that colleges prescribe are the following:

1. A certain number of units in residence. Units are the credits you receive for taking courses. Units in residence are units you take at that particular college. They must add up to approximately one quarter of the units required to graduate.

2. You must follow the curriculum (courses outlined) for your major.

3. You must achieve a minimum grade point average which normally is a 2.0 or a 'C' average.

4. You must show your proficiency in basic computational or mathematics, writing and/or reading skills, and oral communication. Competency can be demonstrated by meeting satisfactory scores on standardized tests, or by taking

appropriate courses, or may be waived with high scores in college admissions tests (Scholastic Aptitude Test or the American College Testing Program).

REQUIREMENTS FOR ASSOCIATE DEGREES AND/OR TRANSFERRING TO A FOUR-YEAR INSTITUTION

An associate degree takes sixty semester units or ninety quarter units. Both the A.A. and A.S. degrees require a certain number of units (twenty to forty) in particular fields or subjects to fulfill your general education requirements. General education is required of all students who wish to obtain a degree. Thus, students intending to transfer to a four-year college will also be required to complete general education courses. The specific courses, categories and number of units of general education may vary according to your academic goal. A.A., A.S. and transfer requirements have similarities but may also have differences. This makes it difficult for new students who have not yet decided why they are in school and what they expect from school. To make the matter more confusing, requirements also differ from one college to the next. Again, I recommend that you see your college counselor and not only buy, but read, your college catalog.

In addition to general education, you will need to complete a prescribed number of courses in your major field of study. This will include some basic introduction courses in your major, and sometimes courses that are in another field related to your major. For instance, science majors usually are required to take math courses such as calculus, and other science courses not in their specific field.

If your end goal is a bachelor's degree, your first two years of college, whether you attend a two-year or four-year, will include thirty to forty units of general education and ten to thirty units of courses in your major. A bachelor's degree requires 120 semester units or 180 quarter units.

GENERAL EDUCATION

The purpose of general education, as you may have heard many times, is to provide you with well-rounded skills and knowledge. Well-rounded means that you have taken courses in a variety of fields which have stimulated your intellectual curiosity, increased your objectivity, opened your mind and provided you with confidence in your capacity to reason.

A major goal of general education is to teach you to think critically. The definition of critical thinking is: *the ability to define an issue or problem, clearly analyze its elements, distinguish relevant from irrelevant information, tell the difference between a theoretical and an actual problem, recognize assumptions embedded in what you read or write, develop an extended line of reasoning to support your answer or conclusion, and enter sympathetically into the reasoning of others.* Conditions for the development of critical thinking include: intellectual curiosity, objectivity, being broad minded, analytical ability, skepticism, honesty, persistence, decisiveness and respect for other viewpoints. Typical general education courses fall under these categories:

COMMUNICATION: Courses designed to help you think logically, to express yourself clearly and concisely, and to understand your textbooks and lectures. Many institutions require or encourage courses in verbal communication such as public speaking or interpersonal communication. Other courses in this category are: English Composition, Expository Writing, Logic, and Argumentation and Debate. Employers seek people who know how to question, have attained a broader perspective on problem solving and who can communicate both verbally and in writing.

SCIENCE AND MATHEMATICS: Often referred to as the hard sciences, these courses will help you understand the relationship between human beings and their environment. By studying the sciences you take part in the intricate, step-by-step processes of research and evaluation and become more critical in your own analysis of daily events in the world in which you live. You use objective factors and rely on empirical evidence rather than subjective factors to make judgements and to reach conclusions. Courses include physical and biological sciences, mathematics, statistics and computer science.

ARTS AND HUMANITIES: The curious student will seek answers by asking how, when, where, and who. Humanities courses help open your mind. They help you to understand the way humans think, behave and express themselves through exposure to various cultures, art forms, music, languages, philosophies and religions. You learn to appreciate our past as well as our present, and to understand differences in people. With the rapid changes in our society and the world at large, the ability to judge without bias or prejudice is a virtue.

SOCIAL AND BEHAVIORAL SCIENCE: In order to keep you abreast with the history of your own country, this requirement usually includes a course or courses covering American Institutions (U.S. History and Government). In addition, you choose courses from a wide range of social sciences, such as anthropology, economics, psychology, sociology, and geography. Social or behavioral science courses are designed to help you understand how people function in society. In psychology you study the individual mind, whereas in sociology you concentrate on groups of people, and in economics you examine people as part of system. Together with the hard sciences, you also learn to rely on objective rather than subjective factors to make judgements or decisions.

SELF-DEVELOPMENT: Some colleges are now requiring a category designed to help individuals understand their own development as physiological and psychological beings. Courses include health, nutrition, career and personal exploration, and life management.

The number of courses in each category will depend on the degree for which you are striving (an associate or a baccalaureate), and which college institution you attend. A list of specific requirements may be obtained from your counselor, and the college's catalog.

FOUR-YEAR INSTITUTIONS

You must apply and be accepted to the four year institution before you may attend. Application requirements include a minimum grade point average, standard scores on college admission tests, such as the SAT and ACT, and particular college preparatory high school requirements, including the high school diploma. If you do not meet these minimum requirements, you may make up these deficiencies at the community college, follow a transfer program as described above and transfer to the four-year institution. Some key points to remember are:

1. Not all community college courses will count or be transferable to the four-year college.

2. The four-year school will accept a limited number of units from the community college. In California the limit is seventy semester units.

3. In California, if you were not eligible to attend a four-year college and are transferring from a two-year college, you must have a minimum of fifty-six transferable semester units.

4. The courses you take at the community college are under-division (freshman and sophomore) courses.

5. You must apply and be accepted to the four year institution. Not all four year institutions are the same.

PLANNING YOUR EDUCATION

Education is not only a means to an end — your degree or career — but also a process. When planning your education don't be too hasty in choosing a major. Be sure that you will enjoy and appreciate the process. I realize many students do not view the educational process as something to enjoy, but it is silly to make it a drudgery. When planning your education, consider this: What do you expect from your education? What specific skills do you hope to acquire? What type of personal qualities and habits do you hope to develop? What interests and activities besides course work do you plan to pursue in college? Remember: your college education is a process encompassing you as a whole person, and takes up at least four years of your life. Make it a rewarding and eventful time.

CHOOSING MAJORS

Many students enroll in college without having a major field of study. Many of these students enroll in career planning courses in hope to find a major. Students without majors frequently feel pressured to choose a major in fear of getting behind the crowd or wasting time floundering at school.

Having a major is certainly important, but for those of you who are undecided, take the opportunity to investigate and explore the options available to you. General education courses are usually introductory courses into a major field of study and offer an overview of the subject. One way of exploring different majors is to take courses that are called "introduction to," "survey of" and "principles of." Freshmen and sophomores have time to explore and consider different fields; however, it is important to be active in your exploration. Visit the departments in which you are interested. Find out what courses you need to take for the major(s). Read the course descriptions in the catalog. Talk to students and professors, and even alumni of that major. Find out not only, how they like(d) the major, but what they plan to do, or have done after graduating. This is true investigation. Get more than one person's opinion on the subject. It is important not to pressure yourself into a decision, or do inadequate investigation.

While exploring possibilities for majors, consider the schools or major fields that your institution has. Notice how the majors are grouped together into schools or divisions. You can get some idea of your interests by deciding which schools interest you the most. Use Table 4 — Holland's Personality Types and Occupational Environments — to help you match your interests to possible majors.

One last thing you may want to consider is whether you would prefer a major in a technical field or a major in a more general field.

TECHNICAL MAJORS: Majors that require courses in specific or applied areas are considered technical fields. The courses typically provide skills and knowledge that may be used in one or a few related occupations. Some examples are: engineering, computer science, music, art, accounting, fire science, nursing, court reporting, and architecture.

LIBERAL ARTS: Science, humanities, social sciences and some business majors are considered the liberal arts majors. The idea behind a liberal arts education is to train students in interpersonal skills, self-management, and critical thinking. Interpersonal skills include leadership, problem-solving and communication. Self-management includes time management, organization, and decision making skills. The uses for critical thinking skills have been discussed extensively in this chapter. The liberal arts student develops the basic skills necessary for a wide variety of management or leadership positions, and will have the background to enter many fields of employment. Liberal arts students are primarily trained in the transferable skills. When you begin to explore occupations you will find that job requirements are similar to skills developed through your general education courses. With basic skills, such as good oral and written communication, interpersonal skills, critical thinking and self- management, you show the employer that you are an excellent candidate for employment. The specific knowledge necessary for your position can be learned on the job.

Students who cannot decide on a special interest, those who want to remain flexible, or those who happen to like a subject that does not appear to be directly related to a career, are wise to stay with a liberal arts major. It's important to enjoy what you are doing at school because it will keep you motivated and will encourage success. Your liberal arts education provides a focus aside from your expertise in your major subject. Figure 3 - Skill Categories & Organizational Structure by Holland Type - describes and categorizes the uses of liberal skills in a work setting.

Employers are not seeking only students who have acquired high marks in their specific field. An employer seeking an accountant, for instance, would rather hire a student who is educated in the arts and has some training in accounting than an accounting major with a 3.9 grade point average but background in nothing else. Companies are also looking for personality types. They seek highly motivated students who are leaders on campus. Many recruiters prefer applicants with liberal arts majors in political science, philosophy, the sciences and humanities because these students have learned how to question and have a broader perspective on problem solving. Unless you are aiming for a technically oriented field, your strongest seller to the employer is lack of specialization. Employers are seeking those with highly needed transferable skills that are the backbone of all job functions. Employees need to become flexible with their skills in order to keep up with the fast changing conditions of today's work force.*

ALTERNATIVE EDUCATION

As more adults enter educational institutions, schools will have to flex to fit their needs. Community colleges, in California, offer night, weekend, and televised courses. In some schools, night enrollment exceeds day enrollment. Private colleges also modify their programs to accommodate adult students by offering evening, weekend courses, or by bringing the course into companies. Other non-traditional alternatives for those who do not have the time to attend traditional colleges are: correspondence courses, credit by exam and credit for life experience.

With correspondence courses, you work independently, using textbooks and a workbook. You communicate with your instructor by letter and mail your assignments. You have approximately a year to complete a course. This type of study is useful for those with self-discipline and those who would like to speed up the education process by taking extra courses that can be completed during free time, holidays, and weekends. Not all institutions accept correspondence courses. Therefore, check with your college or university to insure that your course will count towards your degree. For more information, write for:

THE INDEDENDENT STUDY CATALOG
THE NUCEA GUIDE TO INDEPENDENT STUDY
THROUGH CORRESPONDENCE INSTRUCTION
4th Edition
Peterson's Guides, Princeton, New Jersey

College Level Examination Program (CLEP) are examinations offered through the College Entrance Board. The Board does not grant credit, but sends scores to your college or university who will, in turn, grant you credit.

There are general and subject examinations. The general exam covers English composition, mathematics, natural sciences, humanities and social science/history. The subject exams cover 47 subjects in business, dentistry, education, humanities, mathematics, medical technology, nursing, sciences and social sciences. For more information write to:

CLEP, College Board, Dept C, 888 7th Ave., NY, NY 10019

GUIDE TO CLEP EXAMS,
College Board Publications
Dept. B10, Box 886, NY, NY 10101-0886

---

*U.S. News and World Report, April, 1988.

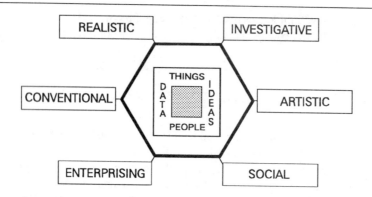

REALISTIC	INVESTIGATIVE
CONVENTIONAL	THINGS / DATA / PEOPLE / IDEAS	ARTISTIC
ENTERPRISING	SOCIAL

REALISTIC

DEPARTMENTS: *Manufacturing, Operations, Production*

Technical/Mechanical Ability:
☐ Precision work with tools, operate machinery
☐ Use body coordination, manual dexterity

INVESTIGATIVE

DEPARTMENTS: *Technical Design, Research & Development*

Research & Investigative Ability:
☐ Seek specific knowledge/information
☐ Conceptualize/synthesize things & ideas
☐ Solve problems and find solutions

CONVENTIONAL

DEPARTMENTS: *Shipping & Receiving, Accounting and Finance*

Technical/Organizational Ability:
☐ Order & retrieve data, as in cataloging, accounting and computer operation

ARTISTIC

DEPARTMENTS: *Research & Development, Design, Advertising, Public Relations*

Design and Creative Ability:
☐ Imagine future, create plans,
☐ Invent new or improvise on old
☐ Illustrate, express ideas

ENTERPRISING

DEPARTMENTS: *Sales, Marketing, Management*

Leadership & Persuasive Ability:
☐ Use persuasive skills to sell, negotiate, promote
☐ Use leadership/management skills to supervise, direct people/groups

SOCIAL

DEPARTMENTS: *Human Resources, Management, Training & Development*

Human Service & Relations Ability:
☐ Use interpersonal/communication skills to teach, provide hospitality, resolve conflicts, advise, mediate and motivate

Figure 3. SKILLS CATEGORIES & ORGANIZATIONAL STRUCTURE
BY HOLLAND TYPE

You can receive credit for your life experience whether it be work or volunteer experience, previous non-credit course work, or knowledge from personal reading. The procedure for receiving credit involves identifying and carefully documenting what you have learned and how you have acquired this knowledge. Your experience must fit subject matter taught in existing college courses. To receive credit you must first find a college institution that offers credit for life experience. Some community and private colleges have such services. Be sure that the institution from which you receive your degree will accept these life experience credits. For more information on credit for life experience, CLEP and correspondence courses write for:

BEAR'S GUIDE TO EARNING
NON-TRADITIONAL COLLEGE DEGREES
by John Bear, Ph.D.
Ten Speed Press, P. O. Box 7123, Berkeley, CA 94707

TYPICAL SERVICE ORGANIZATIONS:

COUNSELING OR STUDENT DEVELOPMENT: There are three types of counseling services offered: academic, career and personal. The services may be offered under one roof, as is provided through community colleges in California. The services may also be housed separately. Academic counseling is sometimes located in each school and/or department. A centralized academic advising area may be offered to students without a major. Experts will help you with courses to take for your major and for general education, graduation requirements, and with academic policies such as probation. Career development services help students plan their career and decide on a course of action to meet their goals. Services generally include: vocational interest testing, a career library, individual career counseling, career and/or job placement. Professional counselors are also available for assistance with personal-social problems. Groups and workshops may be offered in difficult life skills or common problem areas. Short term counseling is emphasized, and students with more serious difficulties may be referred to professionals in the community.

LEARNING CENTERS: The focus of learning centers may vary widely. Originally these centers offered help to students who need improvement with basic skills. Many learning centers today offer a wide range of services from subject tutoring, to workshops on study skills and how to survive college. These services are normally available to all students.

STUDENT HEALTH: Larger institutions will offer basic health services on campus without charging or for a minimal fee.

FINANCIAL AID: Forms for financial aid are funneled to these centers through the federal government. Aid available is standardized by state. Eligibility is determined by parents' tax forms, when the student is claimed as a dependent, or by his or her own tax forms when the student is not claimed as a dependent. Scholarship information is also provided. Various grants, loans and work opportunities may be available.

EQUAL OPPORTUNITY PROGRAM OR STUDENT AFFIRMA-TIVE ACTION: Students who traditionally have been unsuccessful in higher education are sought out, and guided toward academic success. Typical services are: tutoring, financial aid, loans, priority registration, academic counseling and academic monitoring. Eligibility is normally determined during the application process.

DISABLED STUDENTS SERVICES: Services typically include: readers and note takers, tape recorders, braille equipment, and transportation to and from classes.

VETERAN SERVICES: This is the center for handling administration of veteran academic benefits. Academic counselors may also handle this service.

INTERNATIONAL CENTER: Institutions with a large portion of international students may have a center for students to convene, receive counseling/advice, exchange information. It may also serve as a center for host students and faculty to learn about other cultures and to apply for education abroad.

HOUSING: This office provides information and applications for dormitories, or on campus housing. May also provide lists of individuals offering or seeking housing.

CHILD CARE CENTER: These centers have a dual purpose: to offer convenient and inexpensive child care for students and employees, and to serve as an educational center for students learning about child development.

ASSOCIATED STUDENTS: Activities include: student government, clubs and organizations, student activities, and intramural sports.

SPECIAL POPULATIONS: Services and organizations to special populations will vary, for instance, senior citizens, women, reentry students, ethnic or cultural groups, and displaced workers or homemakers.

Smaller colleges frequently provide many services under one umbrella. For instance, financial aid, veterans' center, disabled student center and international students may all fall under student development. Each institution has its own name for its services, and may or may not resemble the titles in this book. The college catalog will list all these organizations along with academic policies/procedures, graduation requirements, a listing of courses offered and the institution's faculty.

DEFINITIONS OF COLLEGE JARGON

APTITUDE TEST: These are frequently used to determine your potential for success in college. Tests required for entrance to undergraduate four-year institutions are the American College Test (ACT) and the Scholastic Aptitude Test (SAT). These tests are normally taken during your junior year of high school. Graduate and professional schools may also require an aptitude test. For instance, law schools require the LSAT, medical schools require the MCAP, and other graduate programs require the Graduate Record Exam (GRE).

CERTIFICATE: A document issued to an individual completing a course of study not leading to a diploma. Certificates at the two-year college require courses in a particular field of study and do not include general education courses. Certificates at the four-year institution are normally granted after the completion of a bachelor's degree and show that the individual completed additional prescribed courses in a specific field.

COURSE LOAD: The number of units a student takes each semester or quarter. Semester System: The course load for a full time student ranges from twelve to eighteen units, with fifteen as the average. Average for a three-quarter time student is nine units. A student is considered part- time when taking six units or less. Quarter System: The course load for a full-time student ranges from twelve to sixteen units. A part-time student will carry less than twelve units. The course loads for graduate students differ from that of undergraduates.

CREDENTIAL: A document showing that an individual has qualifications in a particular field, as in teaching credential.

DEGREE: The academic title given by a college or university to a student who has completed a course of study. Two-year degrees are the associate of arts (A.A.) and associate of science (A.S.). The most typical four year degrees are the

Bachelor of Arts (B.A.), Bachelor of Fine Arts (B.F.A.), Bachelor of Music (B.M.), and Bachelor of Science (B.S.). Baccalaureate degree and bachelor's degree may be used interchangeably. Graduate programs offer both master's and doctorate degrees. Master's degrees are granted to individuals who have at least one year of prescribed study beyond the bachelor's degree. Typical degrees include the Master's of Art (M.A.), Master's of Science (M.S.) and Master's of Fine Arts (M.F.A.). Doctorate degrees are the highest academic degrees granted and normally require at least three years of study beyond the bachelor's degree and include advanced research in a particular field of study leading to a dissertation or book. Professional schools such as law or medical schools may not require a dissertation, only the specialization and advanced studies in the particular field. Some typical degrees include the Doctor of Philosophy (Ph.D.), Doctor of Education (Ed.D.), Doctor of Medicine (M.D.), and Doctor of Laws (J.D.), Doctor of Dental Science (D.D.S.)

DEPARTMENT: A division of the school or institution which houses one or more major fields of study. For instance, the Art Department may have a major in General Art, Art History and Fine Art. Sometimes major and department are used interchangeably.

GENERAL EDUCATION: Courses required by college institutions during the early years of study and designed to provide the individual with basic skills and general knowledge of several fields.

GRADE POINT AVERAGE (GPA): The average of the grades you have received in your courses. Typical point system: A = 4.0; B = 3.0; C = 2.0; D = 1.0; and F = 0. It is used in determining eligibility for financial aid and other benefits. A minimum grade point average will be required for entrance to college, for acceptance into a department or school, for transferring from one college to another and for continued enrollment in college.

GRADUATE STUDY: Specialized study beyond the bachelor's degree leading to a certificate, master's degree or doctorate degree in a particular field.

LOWER DIVISION: The first two years of full time study in a college institution; freshman and sophomore years.

MAJOR: The academic area or field of study in which the student specializes. The major will require a specific number of units: Approximately twenty are required for the two-year degree and approximately forty for the four-year degree.

MINOR: The academic area or field of study in which a student may concentrate in addition to his major. The minor does not need to be related to the major. The requirements will include at least a minimum number of units and sometimes specific courses of study. The number of courses and units will be less than required for the major.

PREREQUISITE: Courses or other requirements that are to be completed prior to a student enrolling in an advanced course.

QUARTER: The division of a school year into four parts consisting of about ten to twelve weeks each. Quarters are designated as fall, winter, spring and summer. A full academic year consists of three quarters, and three quarters is equivalent to two semesters. The summer quarter in this system is the same as summer school.

SEMESTER: The division of a school year into two equal parts consisting of fifteen to eighteen weeks each. Semesters are designated as fall and spring. Institutions on the semester system will also offer summer school courses. The descriptions in this book are based on the semester system.

SERVICE ORGANIZATION: Programs or services offered by the college institution for its student body.

TRANSFER: Changing from one college institution to another one, such as moving from a two-year institution to a four-year institution. Transfer courses are those that will be accepted from one college to the next. Certain courses in the community college are not accepted at the four year college, such as, courses used to acquire basic skills in math, reading and writing, English as a second language, certain courses leading to a vocational certificate; courses for enhancing vocational skills; and courses designed to fulfill high school course deficiencies. The numbering system of courses at a two-year institution is designed to show what is transferable to the four-year institution.

UNDERGRADUATE: Coursework completed towards a baccalaureate degree. Slang: A student studying for a baccalaureate degree.

UNITS: Credit received for courses taken in a college institution. In the semester system, one unit equals one hour of class time for each week of the semester (fifteen to eighteen weeks). A typical semester course is three units, or three hours per week. Courses with labs or studio time may require more hours. In the quarter system, a typical course is four units per quarter, and a typical class meets three hours per week for each week of the quarter (ten to twelve weeks). The semester system requires approximately 120 units to graduate with a bachelor's degree. The quarter system requires approximately 180 units to graduate with a bachelor's degree.

UPPER DIVISION: The last two years of study towards the bachelor's degree; juniors and seniors.

EXERCISE 12 - EDUCATION PLAN

Part A:

1. List all the requirements for two majors you are considering. Indicate the course number as well as the course title. You want to know what it is you are taking. For example, Social Science 216 - Behavioral Science Statistics. List any prerequisites (courses to be taken before you may take your class of choice) for each course.

2. List five specific occupational titles for each major.

3. Discuss the pros and cons of these majors in terms of your interests, values, personality and skills.

4. At this time, which major would you choose? Why?

Note: If you already have a major, list only the requirements for one (your) major.

Part B:

Make an appointment to see an academic counselor at your college to understand the general education requirements for the degree you intend to pursue. Make a list of tentative courses you intend to take to fulfill these requirements.

Part C:

Schedule both your major and general education requirements onto a two year plan. Indicate each course as GE for general education, E for elective and an abbreviation for the major or minor. Remember, some courses will double-count: for general education and toward your major.

SMITH FAMILY

Exercise 12 - Education Plan

ANNE:

Part A

1.   Associate of Arts in Small Business Management:
Major requirements:
Business 170 - Principles of Small Business Management
Business 171 - Business Plan for Small Business
Accounting 025 - Small Business Accounting
Business
101 - Business Law
120 - Principles of Management
125 - Introduction to Human Resources
Electives:
Computer Information Systems 130 - Introduction to Data Processing
Marketing 172 - Advertising and Selling for Small Business
        (prerequisite Business 170)
Management 027 - Tax Preparation for Small Business
        (prerequisite Accounting 025)
Business 175 - Fundamentals of Import-Export
TOTAL = 30 units

2.   Owner of small retail or service business, Manager of small retail or service business, Assistant Manger or Manager in larger retail or service business, Store Buyer, Store Administrator

3.   **Pros**: I chose this major because I can obtain a degree in only two years, many of the classes are practical rather than theoretical, and it is geared for exactly what I want: to run my own antique business.

(Continued)

SMITH FAMILY - Continued

The skills I would gain from these courses would also be useful for managing or running a business that wasn't my own, or in an entry level management position in a store or service business. The knowledge and experience I already have in antiques buying, selling and refinishing would serve as practical experience. I most likely will need to work for someone else to gain more experience. This may be possible on a part time basis as I attend school. It matches my personality because I like organizing, interacting with different people, buying (I'm not sure about selling), and negotiating (when I really see something I like). I would love the traveling, and just being around people who are interested in what I'm interested in. Values and life-style: I am afraid that running a business will be more consuming, and not give me the free time I am used to for household and family things.

Part B

General Education:

Natural Science (3 units minimum): Took six units of Biology previously. Social and Behavioral Science (3 units of U.S. History, 3 units of electives): Took U.S. History, Sociology, Psychology, and Geography. Humanities (3 unit minimum): Took two years of French, one year of American Literature, One Year of Art History, and several History classes (Was a History major). Cultural Breadth (3 unit minimum): Will take Art 106, Art of the Orient.

English Language (3 unit written, 3 unit verbal): Took a semester of English Composition. Will take: Marketing 114, Salesmanship as a verbal communication requirement. Analytical Thinking (3 unit minimum): Double Count CIS 130. Units Have: 15. Units Need: 6. TOTAL Units Necessary: 33

Part C

TWO YEAR EDUCATION PLAN:

Fall 88:	Business 170, Business 171, Accounting 025
Spring 89:	Business 175, Computer Information System 130
Summer 89:	Art106
Fall 89:	Business 172, Accounting 027
Spring 90:	Business 101, Management 125, Marketing 12

MARY:

Part A

1a.   Bachelor of Arts in Magazine Journalism:
Introduction to Mass Communication, News Writing and Reporting, Magazine Making and Editing, Magazine Production, Feature Article, Advance Magazine Production, Law of Mass Communications, Journalism as Literature, Research Methods in Mass Communications, Internship. 30 units.

1b.   Bachelor of Arts in English - Creative Writing:
Composition and Literature, Introduction to Fiction, Creative Writing: Short Story, Creative Writing: Novel, Script Writing for Telecommunications and Film, Principles of Literary Study, Critical Studies in Major English Writers, Children's Literature, Women and Literature, Critical Studies in Major American Writers, Literature of Adolescents, plus 12 units in electives.

1c.   Comparative Literature:
24 units from Comparative Lit: Introduction to World Literature, Masterpieces of European Literature, Women in World Literature, Twentieth Century European Literature, American Folklore Studies, Fairy Tales, Introduction to Literary Criticism, The Novel and Motion Picture in Contemporary Literature.
15 units upper division units in either English, English/Creative Writing, or foreign language. I would use creative writing courses.
12 upper division units in one foreign language: Hispanic Literature in Translation, Literary Masterpieces Spain, Literary Masterpieces: Spanish America, Introduction to Literary Analysis.
Minor: Literature and Other Arts, Introduction to Comparative Literature, Masterpieces of Literary Criticism, Women in World Literature, 20th Century Dimensions, Fairy Tales, Modern Folklore. 18 units.

2a.   Magazine journalist, magazine editor, free lance writer, copy writer, critic.

2b.   Writer, technical writer, proofreader, public relations, teacher (with more education).

(Continued)

2c.   Government employee, interpreter/translator, personnel worker, grant writer, media writer.

3.   It's not so much in choosing majors I will or will not enjoy, I'm just not sure that I will be able to get a job writing when I complete my education. Most of the occupations I listed above sound great, except maybe government employee or grant writer. But how many writers are there making a living? In terms of a major, Journalism seems more practical, but maybe too specific. What if I don't end up working for a magazine? The English major in Creative Writing seems more general and enjoyable, but how practical is it? A major in Comparative Literature would provide a very broad base of courses from which I could choose as well as several career directions. If I specialize in a foreign language I could probably get a job working abroad, or even study abroad! The major or minor in Comparative Culture looks like the kind of major that may better prepare one for anything, like something to fall back on in case writing doesn't pan out.

I'm just not sure I want to study literature or writing. All majors are interesting to me. They fit my personality because I'm introverted (like to keep my head in a book), I'm imaginative, creative and analytical. I also have three years of high school Spanish. I would not like to work under pressure or deadlines, but I guess I would have to. I would enjoy independence. As far as values go, I would like the life-style that goes with writing — sort of do your own thing, make your own rules. I would not mind being a starving artist for a while, but not forever. I'd want some security. But I would not be that dedicated that I'd be a waitress or something for ten years before anything was published.

(Continued)

SMITH FAMILY - Continued

Part B
General Education:
Communication (9 units): Oral: Interpersonal Communication
Written: Freshman Composition
Critical Thinking: Logic
Sciences (9 units): Astronomy, Psychobiology, and Physical Anthropology.
Mathematics (3 units): Math for Liberal Arts Student
Humanities (12 units): Dance History and Appreciation, Spanish 201 and 202,
Introduction to Comparative Literature
Social Sciences (15 units): Required - Government, U.S. History
Electives - Women Studies, Anthropology and Psychology
Self-Development: (3 units): Career and Life Planning
Total 48 units.

Part C
TWO YEAR PLAN:
Completed

Fall 88:	Freshman Composition (GE), Psychology (GE), Spanish 2 (GE), Composition and Literature (EN), Career and Life Planning (GE).

Tentative Plan:

Spring 89:	Physical Anthropology (GE), Math for the Liberal Arts Student (GE), Introduction to Mass Communication (E), Introduction to Comparative Literature (GE), Introduction to Creative Writing (EN).
Fall 89:	Spanish 202 (GE), Astronomy (GE), U.S. History, (GE), Interpersonal Communications (GE), News Writing and Reporting (J), The Novel (EN) or Literature and Other Arts (CL).
Fall 90:	Spanish 203 (GE), Government (GE), Logic and two courses in my major.

SMITH FAMILY - Continued

MIKE:

Part A.

1.　　　Master of Science in Biology
Prerequisites: 1) Undergraduate program similar to that required of a bachelor's degree in biology. 2) Undergraduate grade point average of 3.0 in the last 60 semester units. 3) The Graduate Record Examination Subject (advanced) Test in Biology.

Coursework: A minimum of 30 units of upper division and graduate courses, with a minimum of 18 units of graduate courses. Each program must include six units of Thesis, three units of Directed Research, and two courses from Biology 661- Seminar in Biology, 662-Seminar in Botany, 663- Seminar in Genetics and Development, 664-Seminar in Marine Biology, 665- Seminar in Terrestrial Zoology.

2.　　　Occupations: Fish and Wildlife Biologist, Technical Writer, Forester, Naturalist, Curator.

3.　　　There is no question that I would enjoy this. The question is, how practical is it for me to go back and get a master's degree in this field? What truly are the job opportunities? And will these jobs pay the rent?

B.　　　No general education required.

C.　　　A two year plan for this degree would be full time schooling. I may be able to do a part time graduate program, but I would not be able to work full time. Graduate work takes more commitment than undergraduate work. If I did go full time, I would take one year of course work, take an examination to advance to candidacy, and then spend the next year or so on my thesis. I would expect, that it would take me three to four years for such a program, since I would have to work.

(Continued)

SMITH FAMILY - Continued

SEAN:

Part A:

1.   Business Core: #Economics 201- Micro, #Economics 202-Macro, #Math 114- Business Calculus, Math 120-Statistics, Accounting 200-Financial, Accounting 201-Managerial, Computer Information Systems 240-Business Computer Methods, #Business 218-Business Law.

Marketing Option (Upper Division): *Marketing 300- Marketing, Marketing 310-Retail Concepts and Policies, Marketing 330-Mass Marketing, Marketing 380- International Business, Marketing 430-Promotion Strategies, Marketing 480-International Marketing, Marketing 490-Consumer Behavior, Marketing 494-Marketing Management.

Management Option (Upper Division): *Management 300- Principle of Management, *Marketing 300-Marketing, *Marketing 380-International Business, *Marketing 480-International Marketing, Management 326-Management & Society, Management 405-International & Comparative Management, Management 253-Management Systems, *Human Resource Management 361- Managing Human Resources in Organizations, Management 454-Managerial Decision Making, Management 426-Management Information Systems, Management 421-Management and Small Business Enterprises.

*Prerequisites
#Already Taken

2.   Business Owner, Sales Rep, Marketing Exec, Sales Manager, Customer Service Manager, Marketing Analyst, Bank Manager, Buyer, Retail Store Manger, EDP Manager.

3.   I like the marketing major because it has fewer required courses. I would like to go into marketing and do sales. I would not want to be stuck in an office.

(Continued)

SMITH FAMILY - Continued

The courses in management look interesting, but there are so many prerequisites. I may try the prerequisites that are marketing courses, take the first management course and then see what happens.

General Education: English 100-English Composition, #Speech 201- Speech Communication, Speech 205-Speech and Debate, #Geography 100- Geography, Biology 105-Human Biology, #Math 114-Business Calculus, Spanish 100-Introduction, Spanish 101-Intermediate, #Theater 100- Introduction, #Economics 201-Micro, #Economics 202-Macro, Psychology 100-Introduction, #History 112-U.S. History From 1865, #Political Science 100- Government, English 302-Critical Thinking, Political Science 311-International Relations, Sociology 301-Understanding Cultural Differences.

C.

Fall 1989:	Accounting 200 (MC), CIS 240 (MC), Speech 205 (GE), Spanish 100 (GE), Psychology 100 (GE).
Spring 1990:	Accounting 201 (MC), English 100 (GE), Spanish 100 (GE), Speech 205 (GE), Biology 105 (GE).
Fall 1990:	Math 120 (MC), Marketing 300(Both), Management 300 (Man) Political Science 311 (GE), Sociology 301.
Spring 1991: Option:	Depends on what I find out during Fall Semester. Marketing 310, 330, 380, 480. Management Option: 253, 326, 451 and Marketing380. And last GE course: English 302!

CHAPTER VIII:

INTEGRATION

Now that you have completed your self-assessment and have explored some educational options, it is time to look at what occupations may fit you best. For an optimal choice you must consider all of the variables discussed in the previous chapters: developmental stage, personality, values, interests and skills. Your particular unique combination of these factors will dictate some career options.

Your growth through developmental stages explains your past. You can learn from your history and you can understand more clearly about things to come. There are some basic differences in the young individual's career concerns and a more mature person's career apprehensions. As young adults, you lack information about different careers because you have limited life experience. It is important for you to explore, experiment and research a great deal. You may ignore fields that you identify with disliked subjects in school, for instance, by not choosing a nursing major because it requires chemistry courses. You may be overwhelmed with making an inital decision and feel pressured just to *make* a decision. And lastly, you will worry too much about wasting time because you are in a hurry to get somewhere. My advice is to take your time, don't pressure yourself, and explore all options. In the end, all education and experience will be useful.

As a career changer, deciding may be difficult because of current life expectations, lifestyles and family commitments. You may view a career change as going back and starting over, which is difficult not only financially but personally. You may also have unresolved conflicts from your youth, life tragedies to get through, or other changes and personal growth issues.

Understanding your personality helps to uncover suitable occupational environments between different fields and within a field. Understanding your likes and dislikes, your methods of operating, what people you prefer to be around, and comparing these specific work settings will help you recognize the environment that will keep you vital. You will understand why you did not feel successful in other environments that were not right for you. For instance, although Mary enjoys clothing and fashion she did not like working a retail job. Mary is reserved, intellectual and creative. What was expected from her in retail, an Enterprising environment, was extroversion, persuasion and aggressiveness. These are characteristics that Mary does not have or care to acquire. It is best for you to go with who you really are, not who you *should* be to fit an environment.

Your work values also define more clearly what work environments you prefer. Your work values reveal your motivators and define what "success at work" means to you.

Personal values are as important in determining occupational choices because they infer a particular life style. Our personal values dictate a life style that will limit the type of work we are willing to do. For instance, if your family is more important than a career, you may choose to stay home and raise children and let go of career ambitions. If you value creativity, independence and pursuit of knowledge, you could spend many years in education before pursuing a career. Or you may give up a secure position with a company to "go out on a limb" and "do your own thing". Or by valuing altruism, you may give up family, financial security, and a home in the suburbs to become a missionary and save souls.

Skills and interests are important because they reflect a career direction. Pursue those skills you enjoy using. In realizing that your skills come from many aspects of your life, and are not just learned at school or on the job, and that they can be used in diverse environments, you are freed from confining yourself to those already familar but confining occupations. Lastly, understanding what skills you have, in relation to those you need for your occupational choice, conveys the steps and time commitment necessary to acquire those skills.

EXERCISE 13:
PERSONAL EXPLORATION SUMMARY

CHAPTER 2 - PERSONAL DEVELOPMENT

Exercise 2 - Childhood Fantasy

Exercise 3 - Autobiography

    1.   Role Models:

    2.   Accomplishments:

    3.   Disappointments:

    4.   Current Life Stage and Major Issue:

CHAPTER 3 - PERSONALITY

Exercise 4 - Fantasy Work Environment

Brief Description

Exercise 5

    1.   Holland Personality Type(s):

    2.   Five descriptive adjectives:

    3.   Five characteristics you admire in others:

    4.   Five occupations based on personality:

(Continued)

CHAPTER 4 - VALUES

Exercise 6 - Work Values Inventory

    1.   Top five work values:

    2.   Five occupations that would fulfill these values:

Exercise 7A - Owning Your Values

Values you share with your parents/culture:

Exercise 7B - Values Identification:

    1.   Top five values from exercise:

    2.   Describe life style you would need to live to fulfill those values.

CHAPTER 5 - INTERESTS

Exercise 8 - Data/People/Things/Ideas

Number in order of preference, 1 - 4:

DATA ☐   PEOPLE ☐   THINGS ☐   IDEAS ☐

(Continued)

CHAPTER 6 - SKILLS

Exercise 10 - Skills Categories

1.   Five best of each skill type:

Personal:

Technical:

Functional:

2.   Skills you need to develop:

Exercise 11 - Interest/Skill Inventory

1.   Ten favorite skills (from inventory) to use:

MAJORS YOU EXPLORED:
FIVE OCCUPATIONS TO RESEARCH:

SUMMARY: From the information above, write a job description that fits you by including all aspects of you (personality, values, interests, skills, developmental stage)

SMITH FAMILY

MARY:

CHAPTER 2 - PERSONAL DEVELOPMENT

Exercise 2 - Childhood Fantasy - To ride horses and to write about horses. To live in the country and have a horse ranch.

Exercise 3 - Autobiography

1.   Role Model, Hero/Heroine: Mr. Russell, Katherine Hepburn

2.   Accomplishments: First Prize in Saddleback Creative Writing Contest. Two years on the Honor Roll.

3.   Disappointments: Being too shy. Losing boy friend to drugs.

4.   Current Life Stage and Major Issue: Intimacy vs. Isolation. Who will like me for me?

CHAPTER 3 PERSONALITY

Exercise 4 - Fantasy Work Environment

Description: By myself, but preparing to discuss ideas with someone who is stopping by soon.
Jotting down ideas. Cutting and pasting on the computer.
An office in my home. The room is lined with book shelves. There are books opened on tables, notes everywhere and evidence of a couple of meals eaten while working. It is already evening.

(Continued)

Exercise 5

1. Holland Personality type(s): Artistic, Investigative.

2. Five Descriptive Adjectives:
   Creative, Independent, Perceptive, Sensitive, Analytical.

3. Five characteristics you admire in others: Creative, Flexible, Bold, Selfless, Intelligent.

4. Five occupations based on personality: Critic, Editor, Fashion Artist, Package designer, Set designer.

CHAPTER 4 - VALUES

Exercise 6 - Work Values Inventory

1. Top five work values: Creativity, Aesthetics, Way of Life, Independence, Intellectual Stimulation.

2. Five occupations that would fulfill these values: Author, English Teacher, Journalist, Editor, Travel Writer.

Exercise 7A - Owning Your Values

Values you share with your parents/culture: Marriage and family, freedom, aesthetics, health.

Exercise 7B - Values Identification:

1. Top five values from exercise: Peace of mind, marriage, wisdom, freedom, creativity.

2. Describe life style you would need to live to fulfill those values.

(Continued)

SMITH FAMILY - Continued

    I would always be striving for understanding myself and understanding life. I would need to have time to read, travel, and observe people. I would need to be able to express my ideas. I would need the freedom to be who I am. I couldn't handle conforming to what is expected. I would like to have a mate who would share my ideals with me.

CHAPTER 5 - INTERESTS
Exercise 8 - Data/People/Things/Ideas

Put in order of preference:

DATA: 3   **PEOPLE:** 1   **THINGS:** 4   **IDEAS:** 2

CHAPTER 6 - SKILLS
Exercise 10 - Skill Categories

1.   Five best of each skill type:

    Personal: Imaginative, analytical, reflective, sensitive, motivated.

    Technical: Writing (editing, grammar), cooking, horse knowledge typing/computer.

    Functional: Writing, organizing, planning, researching, analyzing.

2.   Skills you need to develop:

    Writing, interviewing, interpersonal skills, argument and debate, objectivity.

(Continued)

SMITH FAMILY - Continued

Exercise 11 - Interest/Skill Inventory

    1.   Ten favorite skills (from inventory) to use:

Write, brainstorm, use intuition, read for information, analyze, improvise, visualize, conceptualize, research, synthesize.

MAJORS YOU EXPLORED:

English, Comparative Literature

FIVE OCCUPATIONS TO RESEARCH:

Writer, Editor, Journalist, Translator, English Teacher.

SUMMARY:

From the information above, write a job description that fits you by including all aspects of you (personality, values, interests, skills, developmental stage).

Work at home! Choose your own hours! Must be independent, self-disciplined and able to concentrate for long periods of time. Use creative problem solving to develop ideas. Must have excellent writing and analyzing skills. Occasionally meet with employer to review project. Some travel may be required for researching projects.

(Continued)

SMITH FAMILY - Continued

SEAN:

CHAPTER 2 - PERSONAL DEVELOPMENT

Exercise 2 - Childhood Fantasy: Famous athlete: I wanted to have people look up to me. I wanted to be the best at something. I like being in front of a crowd and people cheering.

Exercise 3 - Autobiography

1.   Role Models, Hero/Heroine: Reggie Jackson

2.   Accomplishments: Several All Star Trophies, Leading Salesman at Stereo Store.

3.   Disappointments: Not being able to graduate college in four years. Not getting an athletic scholarship.

4.   Current Life Stage and Major Issue: Exploration - Still exploring majors and careers. Need to decide whether or not to get serious about school.

CHAPTER 3 - PERSONALITY

Exercise 4 - Fantasy Work Environment

A lot of people around who are working for me.
Making decisions, giving directions, on the phone,
people in and out of my office, fast pace.
Plush office with window high up in sky scraper.

Exercise 5

1.   Holland Personality Type(s): Enterprising.

(Continued)

2.   Five Descriptive Adjectives: Aggressive, energetic, persuasive, ambitious, sociable.

3.   Five characteristics you admire in others: Ambitious, intelligent, adventurous, self-confident, energetic, optimistic.

4.   Five occupations based on personality: Business Executive, Customer Service Rep, Operations Manager, Salesperson, Underwriter.

CHAPTER 4 - VALUES

Exercise 6 - Work Values Inventory

1.   Top five work values: Economic returns, Leadership, Achievement, Prestige, Independence.

2.   Five occupations that would fulfill these values: Salesman, Lawyer, Business Executive, Entrepreneur, Athletic Star.

Exercise 7A - Owning Your Values

Values you share with your parents/culture: Financial security, self-confidence.

Exercise 7B - Values Identification:

1.   The five values from exercise: Financial security, freedom, prestige, power, self-confidence.

2.   Describe life style you would need to live to fulfill those values.

I would need a job where I made decisions and where those decisions would make a financially successful business. I would be respected for my daring and savvy. I would be able spend my time on projects that I thought were important. I would have enough free time to pursue my hobbies and recreation. I would be confident that my decisions would make me and my company successful, and because of my success I would continue to be confident.

(Continued)

SMITH FAMILY - Continued

CHAPTER 5 - INTERESTS

Exercise 8 - Data/People/Things/Ideas

Put in order of preference:

DATA: 2   **PEOPLE:** 1   **THINGS:** 4   **IDEAS:** 3

CHAPTER 6 - SKILLS

Exercise 10 - Skill Categories

1.   Five best of each skill type:

    Personal: Independent, persuasive, extroverted, organized, verbal.

    Technical: Electronics knowledge, salesmanship, computer, C.P.R., outdoor survival.

    Functional: Persuade, plan, organize, interpersonal, motivate.

2.   Skills you need to develop: Management and supervisory, accounting, marketing, knowledge of international trends, purchasing, more computer.

Exercise 11 - Interest/Skill Inventory

1.   Ten favorite skills (from inventory) to use:

    Negotiate, initiate, expedite, mediate, motivate, sell, plan, organize, promote, delegate.

MAJORS YOU EXPLORED:

Business: Marketing and Management

FIVE OCCUPATIONS TO RESEARCH:

Sales Rep, Buyer, Bank Manager, Marketing Analyst, Retail Manager.

(Continued)

SMITH FAMILY - Continued

SUMMARY:

From the information above, write a job description that fits you by including all aspects of you (personality, values, interests, skills, developmental stage).

THE JOB: Plan and organize the work of others. Train and motivate team to work toward common goal. Frequent problem solving and trouble shooting. Work with other organizations.

Qualifications: Two years of college. Excellent communication, organization and interpersonal skills. Knowledge of sports and stereo equipment useful.

Salary and Benifits: $30,000 per year plus commission. Plenty of opportunity to advance.

(Continued)

SMITH FAMILY - Continued

ANNE:

CHAPTER 2 - PERSONAL DEVELOPMENT

Exercise 2 - Childhood Fantasy: Architect. Design homes for movie stars. Or, design and build my own home.

Exercise 3 - Autobiography

1. Role Models, Hero/Heroine: Mother, Beatles

2. Accomplishments: Successful marriage, happy family life.

3. Disappointments: Married before completing college.

4. Current Life Stage and Major Issue: I'm in transition, which feels like starting all over. It's almost as if I have to make up for past unfinished business.

CHAPTER 3 - PERSONALITY

Exercise 4 - Fantasy Work Environment

Description: I am with customers
talking about something we both love in
a very old home or shop filled with beautiful old furniture.

Exercise 5

1. Holland Personality Type(s): Social, Enterprising, Artistic.

2. Five Descriptive Adjectives: Helpful, expressive, tactful, acquisitive, innovative.

(Continued)

3.   Five characteristics you admire in others: Idealistic, persistent, patient, empathic, decisive.

4.   Five occupations based on personality: Customer Service Rep, Supervisor Volunteer Services, Sales (creative), Travel Guide, Public Relations Rep.

CHAPTER 4 - VALUES

Exercise 6 - Work Values Inventory

1.   Top five work values: Way of Life, Aesthetics, Associates, Independence, Variety.

2.   Five occupations that would fulfill these values: Homemaker, Small business owner, Salesperson selling artistic goods, Artist, Interior decorator.

Exercise 7A - Owning Your Values

Values you share with your parents/culture: Marriage/family, financial security, education, industriousness.

Exercise 7B - Values Identification:

1.   Five values from exercise: Marriage/family, financial security, self-confidence, work I love, travel.

2.   Describe life style you would need to live to fulfill those values.

(Continued)

SMITH FAMILY - Continued

I would need to continue to be married to my husband and enjoy the company of growing children, possibly later, grandchildren. We would need to be assured of financial security, thus my husband and I will need to keep up the standard of living we are used to and have left over to travel. I would need to find work that can help provide the financial security and either include or allow for extensive traveling.

CHAPTER 5 - INTERESTS

Exercise 8 - Data/People/Things/Ideas

Put in order of preference:

DATA: 3   **PEOPLE**: 1   **THINGS**: 4   **IDEAS**: 2

CHAPTER 6 - SKILLS

Exercise 10 - Skill Categories

1.   Five best of each skill type:

     Personal: Patient, organized, resourceful, motivated, innovative.

     Technical: Knowledge of furniture, art history, geography, real estate, and bookkeeping.

     Functional: Organize, budget, plan, teach, manage.

2.   Skills you need to develop: accounting, particulars of opening business, such as tax laws, bookkeeping, licenses, etc., how to run a running business, such as purchasing, advertising/promotion, payroll laws, import laws and taxes.

(Continued)

Exercise 11 - Interest/Skill Inventory

1.   Ten favorite skills (from inventory) to use:

Brainstorm, plan, organize, act as liaison, provide hospitality, improvise, visualize, promote, delegate, collaborate.

MAJORS YOU EXPLORED:

Small Business Administration

FIVE OCCUPATIONS TO RESEARCH:

Small Business Owner, Travel Agent, Realtor, Retail manager.

SUMMARY:

From the information above, write a job description that fits you by including all aspects of you (personality, values, interests, skills, developmental stage).

WANTED: Mature individual with knowledge of antiques to run small antique shop. No previous retail experience required, but must be willing to travel and learn business. You must be able to buy, sell and appraise furniture from all periods. Will handle shop administrative as well as personnel duties.

(Continued)

SMITH FAMILY - Continued

MIKE:

CHAPTER 2 - PERSONAL DEVELOPMENT

Exercise 2 - Childhood Fantasy: Being a vet and raising animals.

Exercise 3 - Autobiography

1.   Role Models, Hero/Heroine: Lassie and owner, Ralph Nadar

2.   Accomplishments: Completed college, good job, happy family, great wife.

3.   Disappointments: Not enough time. Did not complete education. Did not leave current job before it became too comfortable.

4.   Current Life Stage and Major Issue: Midlife? Is it too late to change careers?

CHAPTER 3 - PERSONALITY

Exercise 4 - Fantasy Work Environment

Description: I'm outdoors by myself observing wildlife.

Exercise 5 - Personality Checklist:

1.   Holland Personality type(s): Realistic, Investigative and a tad Artistic

2.   Five Descriptive Adjectives: Practical, down to earth, analytical, curious, open.

(Continued)

3.   Five characteristics you admire in others: Unassuming, innovative, genuine, persistent, open.

4.   Occupations based on personality: Anthropologist, Pathologist, Social Scientist, Technical Illustrator.

CHAPTER 4 - VALUES

Exercise 6 - Work Values Inventory

1.   Top five work values: Independence, field of interest, intellectual stimulation,achievement, altruism.

2.   Five occupations that would fulfill these values: **Run my own business**, Planning Manager, Research Biologist, Forester, Park Ranger.

Exercise 7A - Owning Your Values

Values you share with your parents/culture:Marriage/family, financial security, stability/responsibility, prestige, health.

Exercise 7B - Values Identification:

1.   Top five values from exercise: marriage/family, self-confidence, knowledge, freedom, altruism, prestige.

2.   Describe life style you would need to live to fulfill those values.

        I continue my life pretty much as it is. I would, however, need to pursue a field that would fulfill my need to help people and other living things and I would need more freedom in my work, and more opportunity to learn about things in which I'm interested.

(Continued)

SMITH FAMILY - Continued

CHAPTER 5 - INTERESTS

Exercise 8 - Data/People/Things/Ideas

Put in order of preference:

DATA: 1   **PEOPLE:** 4   **THINGS:** 3   **IDEAS:** 2

CHAPTER 6 - SKILLS

Exercise 10 - Skill Categories

1.   Five best of each skill type:

     Personal: Persistent, thorough, analytical, practical, critical, precise.

     Technical: Research methods, statistics, computer programming, zoology, regional planning.

     Functional: Organization, public speaking, technical writing, research, management.

2.   List skills you need to develop: Stronger in research methods, and statistical analysis, more specific knowledge of biology, particularly zoology, brush up in chemistry and math.

Exercise 11 - Interest/Skill Inventory

1.   Ten favorite skills (from inventory) to use:

Observe, synthesize, classify, evaluate, analyze, improvise, conceptualize, consult, research, repair, problem solving, work outdoors.

(Continued)

SMITH FAMILY - Continued

MAJORS YOU EXPLORED: M.S. in Biology

FIVE OCCUPATIONS TO RESEARCH:

Research Biologist, Curator, Forester, Wildlife Manager

SUMMARY:

From the information above, write a job description that fits you by including all aspects of you (personality, values, interests, skills, developmental stage).

SUMMARY OF DUTIES: Incumbents will plan, organize and conduct laboratory and/or field observations on birds of prey in conjunction with the Predatory Bird Group, research wildlife management and propagation; conduct natural history observations in lab or in the field.

REQUIRED SKILLS AND KNOWLEDGE: Previous experience and college courses in the natural or physical sciences; camping experience; field observation skills, familiarity with captive propagation and wildlife management; mountaineering and wilderness skills; ability to work long periods of time in wilderness conditions; ability to travel to remote areas; knowledge of research methods and statistical analysis; technical writing skills; ability to manage and organize projects.

CHAPTER IX:

CAREER INFORMATION SOURCES

CAREER INFORMATION

Career information resources are divided into two categories: printed or recorded, and verbal. Most college institutions have career centers with a wealth of printed or recorded information on career opportunities. The information is provided in books, on microfiche, on computers, and on audio or video tapes. Public libraries also carry these resources.

Another source of information is the spoken word. Ask your friends and acquaintances for information on careers and job opportunities. This form of passing on information, is called "networking." The idea in networking is to use your people contacts. If you don't know the person you need to know for a particular lead, you may meet that person through your acquaintances, colleagues, classmates, baby sitter, hairdresser, or cousin.

Another spoken source of career information is through the process called the interview for information. Instead of waiting until you have finished your education and are looking for a job, begin interviewing while you are still in school. Talk to people who have the career you would like to pursue.

CAREER PRINTED AND RECORDED INFORMATION

The three basic categories are printed, audio and video recordings and computer information. Several systems exist for categorizing occupations which makes it confusing for the novice.

Figure 4 - Occupational Fields by Holland Type will help you find categories of occupations you may wish to research. Allow yourself ample time to browse at a career library, or regular library. Don't expect to find all the information you need during your lunch hour. The resources are expensive and are located in a reference section, so you will not be allowed to take them home. Begin your search by seeking information on general occupational areas. If they don't have information on your particular field, look for something that is related to your field. Most occupational guides have information that is general, national and a couple of years outdated. Therefore, in terms of salary and future trends, you will need to acquire information that is localized and current. Some occupational guides or briefs do have localized information, such as the Vital Information for Education and Work (VIEW). For current trends, I recommend to read your local newspaper, career magazines or publications in your field of interest.

Audio/visual sources can provide more personalized information on occupations. Job biographies are interviews with people about their jobs. Other materials show a walk through the lives of people in their jobs.

Computer resources include information on colleges and occupations, and may also include assessments on many of the areas we cover in this book. The computer will list jobs that fit your preferences. Some systems provide a wealth of information on occupations and are limited on the assessment end. Other systems focus on the assessment and merely list occupations for you to investigate through some other source. The advantage of computerized information is the print out you receive to take home and review at your leisure. Use a combination of these resources to suit your needs.

NOVICE'S LIST OF CAREER RESOURCES

PRINTED:

CALIFORNIA OCCUPATIONAL GUIDES. Covers work performed, work setting, entry and licensing requirements, advancement possibilities, occupational outlook and personal qualifications. Information tailored to California market.

CHRONICLE OCCUPATIONAL BRIEFS. Covers work performed, work setting, entry requirements, occupational outlook, advancement possibilities and personal qualifications.

DICTIONARY OF OCCUPATIONAL TITLES (DOT). Lists over eight thousand occupations with very brief descriptions. The DOT uses a nine digit code to classify occupations. This code is used by several other career information literature as a common reference source.

ENCYCLOPEDIA OF CAREERS AND VOCATIONAL GUIDANCE. This set is divided between a more general volume on planning one's career and one covering approximately 250 occupations.

GUIDE FOR OCCUPATIONAL EXPLORATION (GOE). Provides information on occupational clusters. Covers work setting, work performed, entry requirements and a listing of aptitudes required for each cluster.

OCCUPATIONAL OUTLOOK HANDBOOK (OOH). Information of work performed, work setting entry requirements, licensing requirements, advancement opportunity, occupational outlook, personal qualifications and sources for other information.

AUDIO-VISUAL:

VITAL INFORMATION FOR EDUCATION AND WORK (VIEW). Covers work performed, work setting, personal rewards, entry requirements, advancement possibilities, occupational outlook (local and national), personal qualifications and related occupations. Micro fiche. Updated yearly.

COMPUTER:

CAREER PLANNING SYSTEM - EUREKA. Provides information on work performed, entry requirements, licensing requirements, occcupational outlook, sources for other information, programs of study for training. Updated yearly. Also on micro fiche.

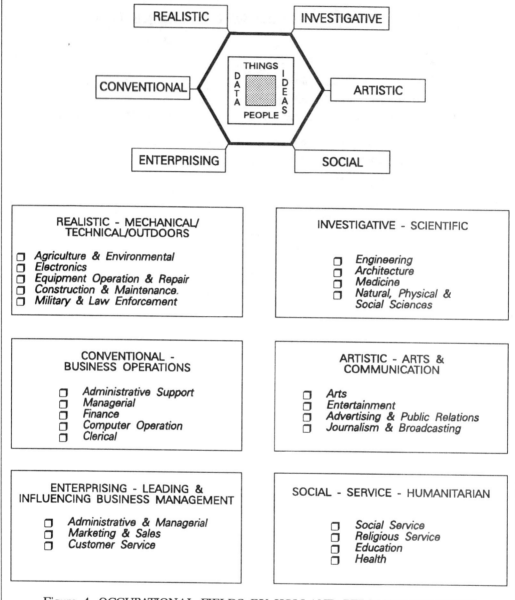

Figure 4. OCCUPATIONAL FIELDS BY HOLLAND PERSONALITY TYPES

EXERCISE 14 - CAREER SEARCH

Investigate two to four occupations for each major you have explored. Answer these questions for each occupation:

1.   To what general field or cluster does it belong?

2.   Describe the job duties and responsibilities, work environment, salary/benefits, and working hours.

3.   Summarize the skills and education required, and the methods of entry into this field.

4.   Discuss the skills you have that are necessary for this field.

5.   Describe the skills you need to acquire to enter this field. How will you acquire these skills?

6.   Describe the pros and cons for each occupation considering your values, interests, skills, personality.   *how is this occupation fulfilling your skills, personality, interests*

7.   Which occupation do you prefer at this time?

SMITH FAMILY:

SEAN:

1.   Marketing Executive is part of a Sales/Marketing cluster in the Business field.

2.   Marketing Executives research market conditions to determine the potential for sales products or services. The executive will establish research and design methods for gathering information and analyze the data to determine trends. They get information on competing companies, previous buying trends, etc. The executive, then, prepares reports that forecast sales and makes recommendations. Salary: $30,000 to $50,000 year. Growth is faster than average.

3.   Skills required: problem solving, knowledge of statistics and research methods, product knowledge, report writing, managing and directing others, analytical skills. Typical entry is with a M.B.A., but they could work their way up.

4.   I can solve problems, manage and direct others, and have product knowledge.

5.   I don't have the research and statistical background, which I would get from taking courses in statistics and research design. I would have to develop my analytical and report writing skills through writing courses.

6.   I guess I'm interested in marketing on a one to one basis. I like anticipating trends for our shop, but I'm not interested in the brainy data research end. I would like to have this information brought to me, and do something with it. Who does that? I don't want to be stuck in an office interpreting data. I'd rather be out in the field and use my verbal skills, not my writing skills.

1.   Salesman in Manufacturing is part of Sales and Marketing occupations, which would fall under a Business cluster.

(Continued)

2.   Manufacturing salesmen sell to businesses or to the government. They analyze the buyers needs, inform them about the product, show how the product will meet the buyers needs, and take orders. Technical Salesmen should have extensive knowledge about their particular industry as well as product, in order to advise on improved materials, how to use these materials and on time or cost saving strategies. They may also train customers to operate or maintain equipment. Other duties include: writing sales prospect reports, checking customers' credit ratings, calling for appointments, and handling correspondence. This occupation normally includes a lot of traveling since workers are responsible for regional territories.

3.   Skills Necessary: Good oral and written communication, pleasant and friendly personality, interest in people, product knowledge, negotiating, ability to gain customer trust, ability to make contacts, good arithmetic, leadership or management skills to go into management position.

Education and Method of Entry: Could work into a sales position with previous experience. However, a bachelor degree is becoming standard. A technical degree in the field of your specialization, such as engineering for engineering sales, is recommended. For non-technical fields a liberal arts or business degree is suitable. Most companies train their new salesmen. Sales experience or related work experience is useful.

4.   I have the basic salesman skills such as the ability to find out what a customer needs, and find and sell him a product. My oral communication is great. Written could use work. I have technical knowledge in stereo equipment, but I'm not sure I want to stay in this area. I think I have leadership potential because people come to me for answers to their questions and for directions. I also like telling people what to do.

5.   As I see it, most of the skills required I could learn on the job. I could learn to write better through writing classes. I could learn technical skills through a technical major. But I will probably major in business and work in a non-technical field.

Continued)

6-7.   My best skills right now are selling and interacting with
people. I am interested in something with variety, fast pace and making money. I
want independence on the job and free time to do what I want. A sales job looks
like it will offer the most independence. I will need to explore these fields in
more detail when I do my interviews for information. I can take some time
thinking this over.

SMITH FAMILY - Continued

MARY:

1.   Journalist falls under a Communications cluster.

2.   Journalists gather information by interviewing, investigating
and observing. They write stories for newspapers, magazines, trade publications,
radio, television and other media. They need to know about local, state national
and international events. They need to be objective as to inform the public and
present differing issues. They may specialize in areas such as sports, fashion,
business, travel, politics or foreign affairs. Reporters will need to travel to
interview or investigate news items, use libraries, and work on computers to
write. This is not a 9 to 5 job. I expect odd hours. Some work can be done at
home if you own a computer. Salaries vary by location and type and size of
employer. Locally, they average $18,000 per year. However, since there is a glut
of qualified persons, the field is competitive.

Specializations: Reporters, editors, columnists, correspondents, news writers,
photo-journalists, copyreaders or news analysts.

Related fields: Public relations worker, proofreader, technical writer, free-lance
writer, newscaster, literary agent, publisher, author, screen writer and critic.

3.   Skills and qualifications include curiosity, sound judgement,
writing skills, precision with facts, research and investigation, organize thoughts
and ideas, ability to work under deadlines, ability to take criticism, and an
interest in a variety of topics. A bachelor degree is becoming the norm for
entering this field. Actual experience in reporting and news writing through the
school paper or an internship is recommended. Entry level positions may include
proofreader, copywriter or facts researcher.

4.   I have good basic writing and research skills. I've won awards for my
writing and have done several "A" papers. I am analytical and organized in my
thoughts. I can work under pressure of deadlines, as I have done to complete
papers (at the last minute).

(Continued)

5.   I can improve on writing skills by continuing to write (papers) for school, find other writing opportunities, e.g. keep a journal, write for a paper, or enter contests. I need to become more objective and see other points of view. Courses in humanities and social sciences may open my mind. I'm not very bold and need to overcome my shyness so I can approach people to interview. An interpersonal communication class may help.

Working on a school paper where I'd have to interview would help. Reading the paper to become more aware of local and worldly events is something I can do, as well.

6.   I would like journalism if I could write about topics that interest me. I'd rather be a critic, but critics don't start out as critics. I'm not sure that I have the competitive edge to go into journalism as a reporter. I see myself behind a desk or at a computer. I prefer fiction writing, literature, etc. I would enjoy researching background information for someone who needs to interview a person. I could write the copy for a broadcaster. I want to stay in the background.

1.   English Teachers could fit under an educational field or service professional cluster.

2.   English Teachers teach courses in composition, poetry, creative writing, literature, grammar, journalism and speech. Teachers must plan and prepare their lessons, correct homework, present lectures and motivate students to learn. Teachers also have departmental and committee duties outside of the classroom. They may meet with parents. They may oversee extracurricular activities, such as publishing the yearbook, or a literary magazine, or school newspaper. English teachers are contracted by junior high, high schools and colleges. Entry level salaries for teachers will range between $20,000 and $27,000 per year depending on the degree earned and geographical location. Currently there is a need for college remedial and English as a Second Language teachers, and a prediction of a need for college level teachers.

(Continued)

Related fields: Drama Teacher, Speech Teacher, Novelist, Poet, ESL Teacher.

3.   Minimum qualifications for teachers include a Bachelor's degree and in most cases a secondary teaching credential which usually includes a fifth year in college. A master's degree is required for community college teaching, and a Ph.D for the four-year college professor. Skills include imagination, writing and editing, knowledge of human behavior, ability to lead and motivate, verbal communication and analytical reasoning, literary analysis, organization, interest in continued learning, reading and research, and knowledge of related fields in humanities. Higher level research skills and frequently foreign language skills are required for college teaching.

4.   I have good writing skills, an imagination, an interest in human behavior (which I can boost by taking Social Science classes). I am good at analyzing literature, movies, plays. Love reading and research. Will get better as I continue with courses. I'm organized in my writing, need to be more organized in my life.

5.   Not sure about motivating others. May learn from education or teaching courses. May volunteer or work in a leading/teaching position and learn on the job. Major Problem: I'm afraid to get up in front of people. Speech class? Will that be enough?

6.   I would enjoy being involved in literature. I'd like to teach creative writing. I'd enjoy being around creative people, encouraging them as I have been, producing a high school literary anthology. I don't know if I'd enjoy disciplining and motivating students who are not motivated. I don't think I'd like teaching remedial English, or English as a Second Language. Although I would not mind teaching English to people from different nationalities. The interest is working with people from different cultures. Teaching literature classes would be great. I need to investigate more occupations before I can choose.

SMITH FAMILY - Continued

ANNE:

1. Couldn't find store owner, but Store Manager would fit under a Business or Retail Cluster.

2. A manager or owner handles or directs (depending on size of store) the buying and selling of merchandise. They develop pricing policies. They negotiate contracts with suppliers. They prepare budgets, and financial statements. They coordinate sales and promotion by preparing displays and advertising copy. They handle customer complaints and customer service. They also hire, train, motivate, supervise, and fire employees.

Managers work long hours. They may work from small retail outlets to major department stores. In the latter, one would move up from Department or Floor Manager into a Buyer or Store Manager position. Benefits may include discounts on store items. Entry level salary will depend and size, type and location of store with the range of $20,000 to 30,000.

Related Occupations: Buyer, Purchasing Agent, Restaurant Manager, Realtor, Sales, Travel Agent, Small Business Owner.

3. Skills necessary are the ability to hire, direct and motivate others, organize information and individuals, analyze prices and market trends, negotiate prices, prepare budgets and financial statements, prepare displays and write advertising copy, handle customers, train, and supervise.

4-5. I have done all these things as a fund-raiser. I have no doubt that I have the skills; it's just a matter of convincing someone else. I need to work on my bookkeeping/accounting, which I can do with a class. I would only need to know market trends for things I currently buy and/or sell.

(Continued)

6.   I would really enjoy having my own shop. I would be okay with working for someone else if I had a lot of independence. I realize, however, that I may need to humble myself in order to learn on the job. The real issue here is not how this occupation fits, but am I willing to take the risk of going into business myself. I know this fits me. I'm already doing it, informally, and love it.

1.   I looked up Travel Agent just for fun. It fits in a business/service cluster.

2.   Travel agents plan itineraries and arrange accommodations for customers. They use computers and reference books to get detailed information on flights, fares, hotel ratings, etc. They also need to know about visas customs regulations, vaccination, and exchange rates. In spite of what people believe, travel agents spend little time traveling. Salaries are low $5 - $10 per hour unless you own the agency. There may be a few benefits such as promotional perks to a hotel or resort. But most of an agent's time is behind a desk, working with customers on the phone or in person, and processing paper work. About one fourth of the travel agents own their own business. Related occupations: Airline Reservation Agent, Travel guide, Ticket Agent, Small Business Owner, Travel Counselor, Tour Operator.

3.   Travel agencies prefer to hire experienced agents or someone who has received formal training from a reputable school. Skills include ability to handle detailed information, and coordinate several tasks at once. Good communication skills and persuasive skills. Knowledge of geography and foreign cultures. Traveling experience in order to recommend and advise. Enjoy people and doing several things at once. Computer skills.

4-5.   I have the coordinating, organizing, people, communication and persuasive skills, again, from my fund-raising experience. I have some traveling experience. I do know my geography. I don't have computer skills, and could get that from a basic course or travel agent school. I'd also need to know about visas, etc.

(Continued)

SMITH FAMILY - Continued

6.This would be another small business owner possibility. However, I'd have much more to learn in this field, and the basic job duties are not as interesting to me as my antique business idea.

MIKE:

1.   Biological Scientists study living organisms from basic life processes at the molecular and cellular level to plants, animals and their environment.

2.   Zoologists study animals, including their origins, behavior, diseases, and life processes. Some experiment with live animals in controlled environments. Others work with dead animals to study their structure. Zoologists are grouped by their interests. In my case, it would be an ornithologist who studies birds. Working environment will vary from classroom, to lab, to field sites. As any scientist, they have particular projects they are studying, such as nesting habits of birds of prey. Most zoologists will be connected with a research institution (university, nonprofit, or government) and have Ph.D.'s. In 1986 those with B.A.'s averaged $19,000 per year, with M.S.'s about $21,000 a year, and those with Ph.D.'s $30,000 a year.

3.   I would need a Ph.D. to do independent research. With a Master's I could work for someone.

4.   They will work independently and as part of a team. They should be able to communicate clearly, have physical as well as intellectual stamina. They should be analytical, patient, observant, know research methods, be objective and have a sense of adventure.

5.   I have all these skills. I don't, however, have the expertise that I would need which I would acquire by going through a graduate program.

6.   This is what I would like to do if I didn't have a family. It would be difficult to get a Ph.D. at my age, not only because I've been out of school, but because I need to work. And I'm unsure that I would get a job doing what I want to do after all of that education. I'm too old to start at the bottom. I would want a position where I could run my own project or study.

(Continued)

SMITH FAMILY - Continued

Questions 1 through 3: Zoo and acquarium careers also fall under the Biology cluster. There are several types of positions, all of which require at least a Bachelor's degree in biology or related field. Because there are many more people interested than there are job opportunities, advanced degrees are preferable. Different positions in this field that I would consider are: curator, zoologist, public relations manager, or visitor service manager. Curators are like collectors. They obtain, identify, research, analyze and preserve collections of animals. They may set these up for displays and exhibits, and manage exhibits. Zoologists provide direction for animal collection and for maintaining records, preparing articles and obtaining permits and licenses. The PR types promote the institution and would need writing and marketing skills.

Questions 4 and 5: I have the management, analytical, writing, basic research skills. I have the transferable skills. I need more expertise in the field. I could get this from coursework and from hands on experience by volunteering, I suppose.

6.   Same as Zoologist. However, I might consider the PR type position. I know I could do that because of my writing skills and enthusiasm for the field.

NETWORKING

Networking is what people have been doing for centuries. People met at the market, social club or the local saloon to swap stories, have a good time and to make contacts. When you need a mechanic to fix your car, or a baby sitter, or a new physician because you moved to a new area, you may go to the phone book, but frequently you ask friends and acquaintances for recommendations. It's advertising through word of mouth.

By networking you are using your resources (friends, acquaintances, or anyone you know) for information on occupations, educational opportunities, and jobs. College students network by telling each other who to take for what classes, what services are available, how they study for tests, or what line to use at the bookstore.

Most people are happy to share with you what they know, or who they know. Don't think of it as an imposition or "using" people, because you will be returning the favor to them. Formal networking is done at professional organizations, social clubs, conferences and conventions. Informal resources are your friends, family and acquaintances. Students should use their teachers or professors as resources for information. Your involvement in extra curricular activities provides you with experience and skills, as well as contacts. Alumni associations are also great sources for contacts.

Exercise 15 - Contacts:

Make a list of fifty people you know who could serve as contact on your career/job search. Include their full name, title, if appropriate, company name and/or type of business or field, address and phone number.

INTERVIEW FOR INFORMATION

The interview for information is an excellent method for acquiring particulars on occupations. Before beginning the process you should have narrowed your career possibilities. After exhausting the career information resources at your library or career center, you are ready to interview. The five basic steps to the process are:

1. To determine what particular occupations you would like to research.

2. To find the right person to interview. Initially it may seem like an impossible task, but it is not. Be creative. Tell everyone you know that you are interested in meeting for instance, a lawyer, a writer, or a veterinarian. You can interview your mechanic, physician, hairdresser, grocer, banker, children's teacher, or accountant. If you are unable to find an interview prospect, look them up in the phone book. College alumni associations are excellent resources.

3. Be sure you handle the interview process in a professional manner. Dress as if you were going to interview for a job. Schedule an appointment that is mutually convenient — you do not want to impose. Make the appointment at his place of employment. Even when you know your interviewee, it will appear more professional in his work environment. In addition, you will see, first hand, the environment in which you plan to work. When it's not possible to visit the place of employment, offer to take him to lunch; pick him up at work so you can briefly witness the environment.

4. Prepare well for the interview. You should not only know about the field, but also something about their company. Have a list of questions prepared. Bring a notebook. The more prepared you are, the better results you will have, and the better impression you will leave. If you plan to pursue that field, or enter employment with that organization, tell your interviewee that you are interested in his company. Ask him about other contacts or resources. People who are content and confident in their job will be happy to help you. Show your interest by asking permission to leave your resume for an internship (on the job training, paid or unpaid), or job opening. You must use tact when interviewing someone about his job. Do not make him feel you are using him, and do not threaten his position with the company. The reason you are there is to find out whether or not you would like that kind of job. If, however, you are intending to pursue a job, then tell the person that you are interested in the type of work he does. Ask him who you might talk to about future employment with that company. A list of suggested questions are at the end of this chapter.

5. Use good etiquette and write your interviewee a note thanking him for his time. If you were particularly enthusiastic about the results of the interview, be sure to let him know.

EXERCISE 16 - INTERVIEW FOR INFORMATION

Make an appointment to interview someone who works in a job that you would like to explore in more detail. Do not interview a family member. Use questions from the list below.

How did you get into this field?

What training or academic preparation did you have?

What do you like most/least about your job?

What are your responsibilities?

Are these duties the same for everyone with this job title?

Describe your typical day.

What personal qualities do you feel are important in your work?

What are the prospects for someone like me to enter your field today?

What advice would you give me to go about applying for and finding a job in this field?

What kind of salary would I expect in this field?

Can you suggest someone else to contact to find out more about this field?

Are there publications I should know of, or professional organizations I should join?

SMITH FAMILY:

MARY:

Interviewed Julie Hart, Author.

1. **How did you get into this field?**

I don't believe there is a typical way into the field of writing. Therefore, my story will be totally different from the next writer. The key to writing is to write. I was a high school teacher and a counselor before I started to write, so to speak. I always wrote for myself. I have reams of journals, travel journals and I correspond with about fifty people. I didn't think of writing professionally because I didn't believe I had talent. Anyway, I first began serious writing after my third year of counseling. I was frustrated because I had so much to share with the students but no time or means to do so. I often recommended simple self- help books to more motivated students. Most self-help books, however, are written for adults. I put together my own ideas on self-help for teenagers. Ideas kept coming to me and before I knew it, I had enough information to do a book.

2. **Was it hard to get published?**

Yes. But when I decided that this book was worthwhile and there was a need, my confidence and my friends encouraged me. It took me two years to find a publisher.

3. **Do you do other work besides writing?**

I continued to work as a counselor for the first two books, and did most of my writing during summer vacations. I'm no longer a full time counselor, but I do part time counseling and some substituting, not only to help financially, but it keeps me in touch.

(Continued)

SMITH FAMILY - Continued

4.   **What do and don't you like about your job?**

I like the independence and opportunity to be creative. I love writing. I like scheduling my own time. However, it takes a great deal of self-discipline to sit down and write every day. When I'm working, I get very involved and intense and could work for hours forgetting to eat and sleep. Because I have a family it is difficult to focus. So I have a very regimented schedule during the day when no one is home. I don't write when the mood comes. I write everyday. I think you'll find that most writers work this way. I dislike the lack of security, being on the spot (people judging her work), peoples' attitudes about writing not being real work, at this point the pay isn't that good (laughs).

5.   **What personal qualities and skills are necessary for your work?**

Besides self-discipline and creativity, excellent writing skills. The best way to acquire writing skills is by doing it all the time, and by reading. Persistence, self-confidence and knowing when to ask for a boost. Research. You must know your topic. Ability to be alone and concentrate for long periods of time.

6.   **What do you think is the best way to acquire these skills? And what advice would you have for me to enter this field?**

First of all, if you want to write, write. Don't think about success. You will acquire the skills by practising. You don't have to major in English or Journalism. However, courses that require a great deal of reading and writing will help. English courses in writing will give you some structured assignments and basic skills. There are several areas in writing you can pursue: proposal writing, technical, magazine free-lance, and T.V. scripts. It is probably best to focus on a particular area and style. While in college, get involved in the school newspaper or literary journal. It also helps to be around other writers. I know you are deciding on a major. My suggestion is to take courses in something that really excites you. You may need to work another job and write during your free time. You can do anything, or decide to work in publishing or journalism so you're "in" the field.

SMITH FAMILY - Continued

MIKE:

Interviewed Robert Bauer, Nature Center Naturalist.

1.   **How did you get into this kind of work?**

2.   **What are the things you like, and the things you don't like about your work?**

3.   **What type of position could I get in the field as a career changer? And how hard would it be?**

As a kid, Bob was really interested in natural history, and was encouraged by his parents. They went camping, backpacking and hiking. It seemed only natural for him to major in the sciences in college. When Bob graduated there weren't many jobs for naturalists, so he got a secondary teaching credential and became a biology teacher. Later, he went back for a master's degree.

With summers off as a teacher, Bob had a lot of time and opportunity to be involved in naturalist programs during summer vacations, sometimes paid, and sometimes as a volunteer. Bob started several programs, and help set up exhibits. He spent more and more time at the county forest preserve, and eventually a "real" position opened up. That took almost ten years.

He likes being outdoors, working with animals, working with the kids and turning them on to natural history. He says he and his co-workers joke about getting rid of the tourists so they can do their work. There still isn't a great demand for this kind of work. He suggested I volunteer, go back and get a graduate degree, learn how to write grants, be open to do any kind of work in the field, and willing to move anywhere there's an opening.

He also suggested teaching at a community college so I'd have my summers free to do my own thing, so to speak. He told me that I could get work, eventually, it just depended on how badly I wanted the change, and what kind of sacrifices I'd be willing to make.

He was real helpful in giving names and addresses of organizations to join, people to contact, etc. I was somewhat inspired, but I'm not real sure how much Anne and I would sacrifice as a family. I also think that I would be more interested in the research end than in what Bob does.

SMITH FAMILY - Continued

ANNE:

Interviewed Linda Browne, Secondhand Clothing Shop Owner.

1.   **How did you get into this business?**

I didn't get into this business by any direct route. In fact, I never thought that I would do this kind of thing. I've had several different jobs over the years. I've done a lot of clerical jobs, because they were easy to get. I've done accounting and bookkeeping. I taught Sunday school, and I did a lot of volunteering when my children were in school. The thing that seemed to stand out, however, was that I always wanted to be the boss . . . A couple of years ago, I helped my husband open his real estate office. I learned a lot. It was actually my husband who encouraged me to try my own business. My partner, a bargain hunter, thought of selling clothes on consignment. Before we opened the store, we read books on consignment shops, we took a course on starting your own business which taught us about researching markets, business plans and such. It was real helpful. Since Jack is in real estate, we had no trouble finding a space . . .

2.   **What did you do to first advertise your business?**
      Where do you get your clients?

We had an article written about us in the local paper. We also advertised in the paper and local flyers. We had a grand opening. After that, it was word of mouth. We attract people because they want to get rid of their own clothes. They usually end up buying more than they sell. Our clients range from older people on fixed incomes, to women who need to go back to work and have a limited budget for a "working" wardrobe. We also get young kids in who quickly tire of their clothes, sell them and when they get checks for $75 and find they can buy several clothing items with that money instead of just one outfit, so they spend their money here.

(Continued)

SMITH FAMILY - Continued

3. **What other things do I need to know about starting a business?**

I'd suggest taking that class I took. They give you all the nuts and bolts. Having a consignment business is like having two businesses; you're both selling and buying. So you need to draw two sets of clientele, and you need to keep both of them happy! But the advantage is that they end up being your returning clients. Location is important. Pricing is important. Sometimes it helps to have an angle, a focus or a speciality, or have inexpensive items to draw people in.

4. **How long did it take you to make your business worthwhile?**

Because a consignment business takes little overhead, it didn't take us too long. Less than a year. We had to learn a lot as we went. We don't accept all clothes anymore. We know how to pick items that will sell. We've learned how to price. And we now know who our clients are. It's important to be aware of your market, and be flexible. Many people fail at businesses because they spent too much money going in, and couldn't catch up to their overhead. And others have this idea of how they want things, but it's not what will sell. You have to be flexible.

5. **Do you think it's better to have a partner, or go alone?**

That's really up to you. If you go it alone, YOU do all the work by your self. Of course, you'd have to pick a partner very carefully. Have everything drawn up with a lawyer. Debra and I are so glad we did that. Business never comes between our friendship, because we know where we stand, and we talked things over thoroughly in the beginning.

6. **What are the pros and cons?**

I like the independence of running my own show. I like working with people. I feel like I'm doing them a service. It's not like selling. Everyone is so excited to get such a bargain. In the beginning it was hard to refuse out of date clothing, and give people their clothes back when they've been on the racks for several months.

(Continued)

SMITH FAMILY - Continued

But, I make my policy very clear in the beginning. We worked many hours, and eventually were able to hire on staff. Because we are a small business, we had trouble attracting and keeping good workers.

Summary: It was inspiring to meet with another woman with similar interests. Linda was encouraging, but realistic. She didn't know enough about antiques to advise me on that topic. Starting an antique shop may be more difficult because the items are more expensive and wouldn't initially draw as many people. Having a refinishing business on the side may help, but that may complicate things. I like the idea of a consignment business, and having smaller, less expensive items. I'm enthused, but realistic.

SMITH FAMILY - Continued

SEAN:

Interviewed Gerald Middleton, Regional Sales Manager.

1.   How did you get into this field?

Like you, I went to college and worked. I majored in political science, and was thinking about law school. But I did so well here, that I kept getting promoted. When I finished college, they offered me the position as store manager with a pretty fat salary.

2.   What do you like most/least about your job?

I like making decisions, working with the other managers, getting people motivated, analyzing competition and thinking of ways to beat them. I'm aggressive and competitive. I don't like long meetings, people who can't follow directions, and the paperwork.

3.   What are your responsibilities?

Everything! I decide what is sold in the stores. I oversee who gets hired, promoted, etc. I train department managers. I take care of advertising and promotions. I develop, track, and evaluate sales plans. I negotiate with sellers to get merchandise. I analyze our competitors. I put fires out. Sometimes I start fires on purpose.

4.   Describe your typical day.

There is no typical day. That's what I like about this work. It's unpredictable. I ususally have a meeting or two. I usually have somewhere to go outside of the store. I'm on the phone a lot. I visit stores.

(Continued)

SMITH FAMILY - Continued

5. **What personal qualities do you feel are important in your work?**

Be aggressive and competitive. Like people and know how to motivate them. Be fair. Thrive on working under pressure and doing several things at once. Be willing to take risks. Be an innovator. Be able to see clearly through a problem to the core. Be able to make quick decisions.

6. **What are the prospects for someone like me to enter your field today?**

For you, they are great. We need more people like you.

7. **What kind of salary would I expect in this field?**

In my position, anywhere from $30,000 and up. Depends on your region, experience, and what you can do.

Summary: Shortly after this interview, I was offered an Assistant Manager position. I think this is something I can and would enjoy doing. But what about school? Although Terry completed his degree, he didn't seem to think I needed to complete my education. He seemed to encourage me to take on more at the shop.

CHAPTER X:

TRENDS AND THE WORLD OF WORK

It is only natural to be concerned that your career choice will also be one that provides opportunity. I would not advise determining your career in terms of job market trends. However, be aware of what the trends are and how they will affect your interest area.

There are three general trends that are influencing the world of work. They are: science and technology, information, and population demographics. Science and technology have created new job positions and whole new industries. As a result of new inventions, most of our working conditions have dramatically changed. For instance, I am writing this book on a computer using a word processing package. Computers may also be used for graphics and drawing, modeling and planning highways, sending original looking form letters to notify students whether or not they have been accepted to college, and for registering for classes.

Technology has dramatically affected our everyday lives. Do you get your money with an A.T.M. card from a computer instead of a teller? Super markets have machines that read markings on the merchandise, record prices, and tell you the total in a computerized voice. Computers have been programmed to perform some counseling tasks, such as academic advising. Computers are used in the classroom in elementary schools.

Several other technological advances are affecting our lives. Think of all the inventions that are new since World War II, such as, transistor radios, color televisions, microwaves, V.C.R.'s, cassette players, compact disk players, personal computers, cellular phones, answering machines, and food processors. These are household items. I haven't even mentioned discoveries in the medical, agricultural, aerodynamics, space technology, and other fields. Two expanding technical fields are bio-technology for discoveries in medicine and genetics, and for finding new strains of plants for food; and materials engineering for discoveries in high performance materials to handle critical design and production problems in autos, aircraft and processing equipment. Six percent of the jobs created between now and the year 2000 will be in high-technical fields and will permeate the economy with jobs in goods and services. Therefore, technical sales and marketing positions will also be in high demand. Salesmen must be able to communicate with the engineers or other technical staff regarding product development, and with the public for training and practical usage.

The information industry also has a major effect on employment trends. We are constantly processing, copying, providing, researching and revising information. We hear it on the radio and television, we read it in printed matter. The shift in U.S. economy is from manufacturing to service and information, which is away from blue collar to white collar work. Manufacturing has moved, and will continue to move, outside of the U.S. All economies are interdependent; thus, we should also be aware of international trends. International finance will continue to grow as our world becomes smaller and more international. The primary industry in the U.S. is information and services, employing seventy-five percent of the population. Because of the advances in technology, such as computers, radio, television and telecommunications, we process, send out, receive, review and discard more information and much faster.

The entertainment field, the traditional home of which was the theater, now comes to your screen at home. We now have television by cable and satellite, and can rent movies. For the population with children, it is possible to view a play, a concert or a sports game on the screen (and not need a baby sitter). Local and global news is brought to your screen "live." Talk shows provide information on worldly events, and also the personal and pathological stories we normally only read about in psychology texts. Numerous "how to" books are a big business in the publishing industry.

Computer and information applications in business create jobs for systems analysts and computer scientists. Computers will also be increasingly incorporated into retailing, home shopping, advertising, accounting, international operations, communications, and telecommunications.

The third factor affecting our work choices and environment is population trends. The baby boom bulge of our population is now approaching middle age, with the eldest members close to fifty and the youngest in their thirties. As this population continues to age, the services typically provided to the older and more affluent will proliferate. Fields such as medical services, travel and leisure, adult education, entertainment, and personal care will be in strong demand. This population is freed from raising children, thus has more leisure as well as money for travel. Devaluation of the dollar has created a sixty percent increase in foreign tourism in the U.S., and has also increased domestic travel. Jobs in the travel and hospitality fields will increase. The median age increase, compounded with growing belief in health maintenance, will intensify the interest in health-related services. Psychological services, gerontology, plastic surgery and sports medicine are some of the particular fields that will grow.

This generation has a different attitude toward work. Jobs are no longer just "jobs." They are looking for careers, challenges, and flexible work styles. The baby boomers are typically more educated and more affluent; they were indulged as they grew up, and believed that their opportunities were endless. This group is also the fastest growing segment of the labor force. Opportunities for mid-management positions will not go to all of those qualified. Thus, the baby boomers are making lateral job or career changes, and many entrepreneurs strike out on their own.

Meanwhile, the 1960-78 baby bust will create a dramatic drop in young workers and will result in less competition for entry-level employees. During the seventies, as a result of the baby bust, many schools were closed and educators lost their jobs. During the 1980's the baby boomers have created their own baby boom, which has ensured a new need for children's services and products. A lack of teachers is predicted for the 1990's.

The number of women in the work force will continue to increase. Currently it stands that about one half of women in the U.S. are working. In the next decade nearly fifteen million new jobs will be created. Eighty-five percent will be filled by women, minorities and immigrants. Women alone will take two out of three of these positions.

The composition of working America will change, as must many of our attitudes about work styles, management styles and education. We will need more flexible work schedules and child care services in industry, more adult education in technical as well as basic skills, and English as a second lauguage. An increase in global and cross-cultural awareness is necessary to stay competitive and work together with foreign nations and to understand the diversities within our own nation. There will be opportunities to use foreign language skills in international finance and international law. Interpersonal skills gained from majors in psychology, sociology and anthropology will also be needed. Technical advances have freed us from concerns with the mechanics of our work. The new emphasis will be on the human issues in the work force.

CHAPTER XI:

MAKE IT HAPPEN

You have discovered several aspects of yourself: your values, interests, personality and your skills. You have reviewed trends in the world of work, and you have looked at occupational environments, in general, and those that may suit you.

Now it's time to make some decisions and set some goals. This may not be difficult for those people who only needed direction, but others may find it difficult to decide because they like so many things, or dislike so many things. And, for still others, the decision isn't the difficult part; it is following through on the decision.

DECISION-MAKING

Decision-Making Process adopted from H.B. Gelatt:

1. **Define Decision**: Before making a decision, you need to understand what the decision is. Several issues may revolve around your decision, and often you have more than one decision to make. For instance, if you are deciding to attend college, you also need to determine what college to attend, what your major will be, and what your course load will be. You may also be choosing between working or not working, and living on campus or commuting. In defining your decision, you need to analyze the sub-decisions so it is clear to you what you are actually deciding. Then decide on each issue separately.

2. **Brainstorm Options**: We tend to consider only a few options because we are emotionally tied up with the decision, or in too much of a hurry to look at all the angles. Think of all the possible options to your situation. Brainstorm options for your decision. Don't just stay with the ordinary, practical and common sense. Be imaginative.

3. **Research Options**: Investigate the information necessary for each option you have listed. You will already have a great deal of information from your personal and career exploration. But do not underestimate the need for this step and make a decision prematurely. Look up facts and figures. Ask those people who have the answers. Make those phone calls. Use your resources. For instance, if you want to go to college, but are unsure about the financial aspect, find out how much it will cost you, about financial aid and scholarship programs. Don't make a decision without the correct information, or from hearsay.

4. **Analyze each option** for consequences, risk, and desire: Consider the consequences both to yourself and others. What are the positive and negative results from your action? Examine the risk(s) involved. What is the worst thing that could happen? The best? If the risk is great, are you willing to gamble? What are the assurances that you will succeed? What is the pay off? Lastly, think of your desire for the option. If you want something enough, you may be willing to take a greater risk and confront greater consequences than you would normally. After writing down the data for each choice, it will be clear that some options will just not be worth the risk or consequences leaving you with a few desirable possibilities.

5. **Time out**: This step is very important, and should never be left out. Making a decision using this process takes a great deal of analyzing and thinking. After researching possibilities and consequences for all of your options you will be fed up with the whole process. Therefore, take a break. Even though you feel pressed to decide, don't force it. Pretend your decision is a job, and now it is the weekend.

Do something that will take you away from thinking about it. Take yourself and a loved one out to dinner. Go shopping. Go camping for the weekend. Read a book. Do something non-stressful. Whatever it is, do not think about your decision. You may dream about it, or different aspects may haunt you. Do not allow yourself to dwell on the details. Be sure to give yourself at least a day, but preferably more time off. Allow your conscious mind to rest while your unconscious mind takes over. Sometimes when you take time out the answer becomes clear. You may have an intuitive feeling, or you will realize that the answer was there, but you couldn't see it through all your details and emotions. If the answer is not clear, return to your paperwork (options) refreshed from your vacation, and look it over. With a clear mind, it will be easier to make a decision.

6. **Make decision and how to implement**: It is not enough just to make a decision. It is important to write down the steps necessary for your decision to take place. Incorporate the goal setting process discussed later in this chapter.

7. **Evaluation**: We are taught that once we make a decision there is no turning back. It is not only permissible, but important to evaluate your decision once its workings are in process. Changing your mind does not mean you are a failure. Not recognizing a wrong decision, or not admitting to a mistake, is failure to be honest with yourself and others. This step is not an out to committing to your decision. It is more like probation at work. Try out your decision on a trial basis. Stand committed, but leave open the possibility that you may change or your circumstances may change, or that you didn't have all the information. Some decisions, of course, will be more difficult to reverse than others. You may not want to reverse your decision at all, but merely alter it. For instance, if the decision was to attend college full-time and you find that you are overwhelmed, you may decide to go part-time the next semester, or you may drop some classes. Write into your decision plans a check point for evaluating how the decision is going. Be sure to formally evaluate how your decision is working out when you planned you would. Then make modifications if necessary.

Exercise 17 - Decision Making

Make an important decision using the format described above. If you are ready to make a decision about your education or career, do that.

SMITH FAMILY:

MARY:

1.   **Define decision.** I want a major that will both be enjoyable and get me a job in my field of interest. I have researched majors and career possibilities in English — Creative Writing, Magazine Journalism and Comparative Literature. It all still appears a little hazy to me. Nothing is definite. Should I choose a major or stay undeclared?

2.   My **options** for a major are the three mentioned above, alone or with a minor in Comparative Literature, or not declaring a major.

3.   **Information and research** on these majors are provided in the Exploring Majors and Career Search Assignments. I have a year and a half before I have to declare a major.

4.   **Consequences:**

Major — I may not like the courses, I may like the courses but they won't be practical when I look for work. I'm not sure what I want to do and may be choosing prematurely.
Undeclared — I want to get going with my life. I may end up staying in college an extra year because I don't decide.

Risk:

Major — I may choose the wrong major and have to change. I may choose a major that won't lead to a job that I like.
Undeclared — I may waste time at school and have to attend longer.

Desire:

Major: I want a major so I can feel like I'm heading somewhere. Undeclared: I want to be sure and not make the wrong choice.

(Continued)

SMITH FAMILY - Continued

5.   Let it stew. I did complete the first four steps to this assignment and discussed all the possibilities with my parents.Over the Thanksgiving vacation I didn't think about school at all. Now that it is time to turn in this assignment, I still don't know what to do.

6.   Make decision and how to implement. I decided not to decide. I will stay undeclared for another semester and take introduction courses, in all three majors, that will also apply to general education requirements. If that doesn't work, I can risk taking a few elective courses. I will also get involved in the school newspaper, and continue to research career possibilities.

7.   By the end of Spring semester I will see if I am prepared to declare a major.

SMITH FAMILY - Continued

SEAN:

1.   I'll be a Junior next year and am still undecided about a major. It will probably be in an area of business. I am doing very well at my current job and have been asked if I would be interested in being a floor manager. That would radically change my working hours. I guess I have two decisions: what should I declare as a major? And should I take this promotion at work? Since the work decision is more eminent, I will work on that one.

2.   **Options:**

   a.   Increase work hours and attend school full-time.

   b.   Do not increase hours and attend school full-time.

   c.   Do not increase hours and school part-time.

   d.   Increase hours and attend school part-time.

   e.   Look for other job and work part-time, or full-time.

   f.   Take off school for awhile and increase hours.

   g.   Increase work hours, decrease school hours and go to summer school.

   h.   Join the navy.

3.   I've researched the possibilities or options "a," "b," "d," "f," "g." I could handle three classes per semester and my work load, and take another one to two classes in summer school. With this schedule it would take me three to three and a half years to graduate. I have also explored having my company pay for my education. However, there is another decision here. Do I want to commit myself to stay with this company or even stay in this business for very long?

4.   **Consequences**

   a. Increase hours and school full-time. No free time. Not enough study time. Would overload self. This is out of the question.

(Continued)

b. Do not increase hours and school full-time. That's what I'm doing now. I would make less money. I would not have the experience in supervising. I would be saying that school is more important than work. I would be able to finish school on time. I probably would get bored with job, or frustrated if someone else would supervise me.

d. Increase hours and school part-time. I would not be able to finish school on time. My parents would be upset because I'm putting work in front of school. They may even expect me to become financially independent. I would make more money and get supervisory experience. I would be committing myself to this field at least for a short term period. I may not have the same opportunities to explore other fields in business through internships due to lack of time.

f. Take off school for awhile and increase hours. Parents would be very upset. May lose interest in school and never go back. Not a good idea.

g. Increase work hours, decrease school hours and go to summer school. Same consequences as option d, except I'd have even less free time, but would complete school sooner.

Risk:

a. Increase hours and school full-time. I'd lose my job, do terrible at school, or become too stressed.

b. Do not increase hours and school full-time. I could become very unhappy at work.

d. Increase hours and school part-time. Parents want me to move out and/or pay for my education. I get too involved in job and let school go. I would not like new job.

f. Take off school for awhile and increase hours. Major trouble with parents. Never go back to school.

g. Increase work hours, decrease school hours and go to summer school. Too much work not enough play, something may give.

(Continued)

SMITH FAMILY - Continued

Desire:

    a.   Increase hours and school full-time. No desire.

    b.   Do not increase hours and school full-time. I want to finish school as soon as possible.

    d.   Increase hours and school part-time. I want the promotion, but I'm not sure if I am grabbing at something too quickly just because it's there and looks tempting.

    f.   Take off school for awhile and increase hours. Be nice to have a break from school.

    g.   Increase work hours, decrease school hours and go to summer school. I could have my cake and eat it too as long as I could convince my parents.

5.   I didn't have a lot of time to think about this because they wanted an answer at work. I went to a party this weekend. I also had to work, but I tried not to think about promotion.

6.   An idea did occur to me when I was talking to a friend: I could try the promotion out on a trial basis from January to August. Maybe by then I would have a better idea of what I want to do, and present it to my folks that way.

7.   I can start new job during Christmas break, take three courses Spring semester, see how it goes and evaluate in April. I can then decide on summer school, and re-evaluate in August. Meanwhile, I will need to explore (through interviews for information) other career possibilities in business.

(Continued)

SMITH FAMILY - Continued

MIKE:

1.   **Decision**: To return to school for master's degree, Ph.D., or somehow make a career change so I can work in my area of interest.

2.   **Options**:

   a.   Quit job and find job in field of interest.

   b.   Quit job and go to school full-time.

   c.   Stay in job and school part-time.

   d.   Go to school full-time and work part-time.

   e.   Drop out of society and do my own thing.

   f.   Organize and lead nature trips during summer months or vacations.

   g.   Take a leave of absence to figure out what I want, or get this out of my system.

   h.   Keep job and do volunteer work at local zoo, or ecological organization.

3.   Am considering options "c" or "d." Let's include option "i," which is not making a change at work but doing options "f" and "h" to pacify me. I'm not qualified to work in field of interest without further education. Explored graduate programs. Most Ph.D. programs require full-time enrollment. Could go part-time for master's degree. Some (expensive) private institutions accept part-timers. Have thought about job sharing or consulting. Could work at local zoo on weekends, but they often start you with very menial jobs, and it's competitive. Ecological society involves political activities which may not look good at work since many of these groups oppose our planning. Ha! However, could join the Sierra Club, or Audubon Society for social reasons, and to go on backpacking trips. Have not explored leading trips.

Have an idea to approach community service agencies through the community college. Unsure of credential requirements, insurance, etc.

(Continued)

SMITH FAMILY - Continued

4c. Stay in job and school part-time.

Consequences:

Not enough time to really concentrate on school. Will have to change leisure life style. Will not look good with employers. Will only be able to work towards master's degree.

Risk:

Confrontation at work regarding my plans. Unable to be a student again. No job opportunities with master's degree. May disrupt home life to major proportions.

Desire:

Want a change and see this as a beginning step. Since I have no clear goal in mind, this may get the ball rolling.

d. Work part-time and go to school full-time.

Consequences:

Financially not feasible unless we dramatically change our life style and Anne gets a well paying job. (Which at this time is not in the picture.) Not sure there is a part-time job that I'd want to do at this point.

Risk:

May not be able to adjust to "being a student." May disrupt home life to major proportions. May not find a job in new field after graduation.

Desire:

Same as in "c," however, desire to attend full-time is not quite so strong at this point.

(Continued)

i. Keep work situation as it is, but get involved in ecology and ornithology groups to appease self.

Consequences:

This would not cause any major changes in my life style, would not affect financial status, etc.

Risk:

No risk, except it may not do the job. I may not be appeased for long.

Desire:

This is a good idea. I will do this regardless of whether I return to school or not.

5.   I took time out for awhile because I was so involved at work that I had no chance to think about it. However, it reinforced in me that I really want out. I don't dislike my work, but I feel restless. I want more from life than this. I guess it's the "mid-life changes" you always hear about.

6.   I'm not ready to make a decision as yet. I want to explore graduate programs in more detail. I want to talk to some people who are working in the field in various contexts, such as government employees (which may be the easiest transition for me), community college teachers, college researchers, field workers, and maybe even a vet. I also need to think about my motivation. Part of the attraction is to be outdoors and observe. I want to get away from computers, desks, and being in the public. Therefore, I need to question whether the change will really be that much of a change.

7.   The plan is to go with option "i," and continue to explore graduate schools and research occupations, and reevaluate or decide in six months.

ANNE:

1.   What kind of work/career should I pursue? There actually are several questions here. Do I want to take just a job that will keep me busy and somewhat satisfied, that doesn't take a great deal of commitment? Or should I go back and get a degree and pursue a career? Or should I try my idea of going out on my own?

2.   **My options** are:

     a.   Not to work and continue with volunteer work.

     b.   The same as "a" with hope to move into a paid position.

     c.   To work part-time in any old job just to keep busy, and keep hobbies as I have been.

     d.   Go to school and get real estate degree, and sell homes.

     e.   Find a job in antique store and work my way up.

     f.   Take out loan and start my own business.

3.   **Research:**

I spoke with directors of a few non-profit organizations about the possibilities of a position for me. I now found out what I would need to get a real estate license and check job possibilities/probabilities. I know people in the antique business, but no openings. I went to a small business counselor to find out about opening a business.

(Continued)

SMITH FAMILY - Continued

4.   **Desire:**

My desire is to develop my hobby into a job. I don't want to continue volunteer work. I am bored with it. I don't really want a paid position, it would just make it better than being a volunteer. I could work part-time in a job, but I would rather "do" something worthwhile, or that truly fit my interest. Real estate could be fun. I wouldn't mind working for someone if I were respected for my knowledge. I'd love to have my own store!

Consequences:

The consequences of volunteer work or just any job is that I really wouldn't be getting ahead, or enjoying my work. The consequence of working for non-profit organization is that I am not really very committed, and so I would probably lose interest. Real estate could be fun, but is risky. Working for someone in antiques could be like working for someone in any job. Owning a business is difficult.

Risk:

The major risks would be in real estate and in owning my own business, for I believe, obvious financial reasons.

5.   I've been putting this decision on hold for several weeks. I've been busy with other things.

6.   I have decided to take some courses toward a Small Business degree, as well as a real estate course. Since Mike and I are both thinking about life changes, we really need to work on this together. I may end up just getting a job to help him go back to school, or going for a real estate position. Or, he may have to wait until I find something I like that will also partially support us, so he can then go back to school. Or, maybe he will change jobs without going back to school. Thus, I've decided to proceed with courses that will help toward my desired goal, and then see what happens.

7.   After this semester I will reevaluate based on what Mike and I decide.

GOAL SETTING

To be successful you must define what "success" means to you. To achieve that ideal, you need a goal. In working toward your goal, you need four key ingredients: motivation, discipline, guidelines/organization and support. All four work together and are intertwined in the goal setting process.

You have reviewed your motivators by identifying your values. Your goal is not only determined by your values, but your values influence the route you choose to obtain your goals. Different factors motivate different people. The things you treasure or find important will serve as rewards as you work toward your objective. Include part of your goal as a reinforcement while you are in the process of attaining that ideal. For instance, if you want to be a professional singer, begin by performing as an amateur.

Closely connected to motivation is discipline. This is the ugly word used to describe housebreaking our dogs or teaching our children right from wrong. Self-discipline, on the other hand, is a beautiful word because it gives us freedom. The definition of self-discipline is training and control of oneself and one's conduct usually for personal improvement. Through practising self-discipline you train yourself for control over your behavior until that demeanor becomes natural.

Freedom is achieved because our desired conduct is internalized and no longer an effort. The desire to obtain a goal, if sincere, will motivate you to be disciplined. Through repeated effort in studying or practising you will become self-disciplined. Include aspects of your goal and rewards along the way to stay motivated.

Now all you need are guidelines and organization. Without these you will not know where to begin. Guidelines provide a step-by-step procedure to work toward your objective. In order to set up these guidelines you need to organize your time and your tasks. Even if you have successfully motivated yourself, have self-discipline and have organized guidelines to achieve your goal, you will need support from others to achieve your goals. There are always going to be those days that you feel like everything is going wrong. Find someone to encourage you along the way. Don't pick someone who, when things get tough, will baby you and do your work for you, or tell you you do not have to go through with it. You also don't want someone to tell you, "I told you so", "be realistic", "get a normal job", "that's life", "you're a dreamer", and "you're too idealistic". You need a coach, someone who will encourage and support you and listen to your woes. She must believe in you. She does not have to agree with your goal, but must support you. Share all aspects of the goal with this person, so she can be up to date, and catch you when you are slacking off. You may even choose a partner and take turns helping each other toward your respective goals. In the remainder of this chapter I will discuss in more detail how to work these ingredients into the planning of your goals.

Are you a procrastinator? Do you set goals, but not follow through and then get mad at yourself? Are you afraid of what lies ahead? Do you hate to plan? Do you fear failure? Is it difficult for you to decide where to begin and how to get somewhere? You are not alone. Before you begin to set goals, you must find out what is preventing you from setting and attaining your goals.

EXERCISE 18A - GOAL OBSTACLES

Make a list of all the reasons why you may not attain your goal.

There may be practical reasons that will make it difficult to reach your objective. For instance, Mike is financially responsible to his family and feels that he cannot quit his job and start all over.

Many reasons for not achieving our goals have to do with our fears. Recognizing and admitting our fears is tough. We are taught not to acknowledge our weaknesses, because conceding to them makes us not okay. Instead, we go around covering up our weaknesses, fooling others and ourselves. Often others can see through our cover ups. Often those we are trying to fool can read between the lines of our behavior and what we say. So, why do we spend so much effort fooling others and ourselves? Because we tell ourselves that it isn't acceptable to be afraid, to not understand, to not have all the answers, and to not be perfect. Challenge these thoughts because they are your biggest barrier toward achieving.

As part of the exercise, write down your fears. When you have completed your list, share it with someone you trust. Instruct your listening friend not to feed your fears, but just to listen.

EXERCISE 18B - GOAL SOLUTIONS

Review the list from Exercise 18A and pretend it belongs to someone else.

On another sheet of paper, list solutions and steps that will help overcome these obstacles.

Brainstorm ideas and challenge your fears with answers. Once you explore prospects, you will discover new avenues for possibilities.

For instance, if Michael wants to be a wildlife biologist, he will need to get a master's degree or a Ph.D. If he is the main support of the family how will he be able to afford to attend graduate school? What prospects are there in the realm of his goal? If he decides not to get the graduate degree, what can he do that is related to his goal?

Is there a leisure activity that will help him either gain skills toward his goal, or be involved in the things he enjoys most? If he chooses to pursue the degree, he has several (uncensored) options. He could divorce his wife and live by himself. He could sell his house, and live on a smaller budget, and borrow money for school. His wife could work for the time it takes him to get a degree. Since she is unemployed, he can wait until she decides what it is she wants to do and then follow through with his plans.

A fear that Mike needs to challenge is whether he'll find a job after all his schooling. He can challenge this fear by investigating career opportunities and trends. He will need to decide what he really wants. If he wants the Ph.D for its own sake, the job in the end won't matter. If he wants to work with wildlife, he may not choose to get the Ph.D. and may find another route toward his goal. He could surround himself with an environment similar to his goal while taking small steps toward his ideal. He could take courses in his area of interest, go on a safari, participate in voluntary agencies for saving endangered species, or work at the zoo. He may even be able to open up his own travel tour business for visiting exotic areas such as the Galapagos.

(Continued)

EXERCISE 18B - Continued

A major agent in setting goals is investigation and exploration. Look for options and alternatives, the more the merrier. After brainstorming options you will consider your values. Does Mike want his present day life-style to continue, or is he willing to take the risk and live in temperance while he pursues his goals? If his relationship with his wife is something he values, he will have to discuss these things with her. Thus, part of goal setting is creating a harmony between your new objective and your existing values and life-style.

EXERCISE 18C - GOAL SETTING

Remember your Fantasy Work Environment (Exercise 2), and find your notes on unfulfilled values (Exercise 7B). In the case of the Smith family, Anne's fantasy is to travel, and be around old things. Mike's ideal is to be a wildlife biologist. Sean's dream is to be successful at his own business. And Mary's wish is to create and commune with others who are as intensely interested in the project as she is.

Combining your fantasies with self-understanding and career exploration, you will match your ideal to real career prospects. By listing obstacles and finding solutions you have both clarified and refined your goals.

You must also analyze what your fantasies mean. What aspect of your fantasy can be defined as a goal? How will you know that you have reached your goal? For example, Mary's fantasy was to write. Is her goal to write, to write and be published, or to write, be published and be recognized? If her goal was to be a successful writer, what steps would she need to take to get there?

Some goals are too far off to plan realistically. A well defined ideal or long term goal can serve as your motivator. But breaking down your main objective into smaller, short term, goals that ultimately lead to your long term goal, will simplify the process. Short term goals also serve as rewards that will encourage you to continue towards your long term goal. In order to accomplish this, you need to understand the key aspects of your goal.

(Continued)

For Mary, the components were independent and mutual creativity, and the opportunity to use her writing skills. What occupations include these factors?

Mary could work for a newspaper, television, or a publishing company. She could write travel brochures, children's books, advertising copy, or speeches for political candidates. If she wants to write, her first step would be to write. If she wants to complete college, one of her first steps would be choose a major. She has already found several possibilities for majors for the field of writing. In order for her to choose between majors, she should talk to the appropriate persons in the departments and to students who are in the major for information. She should also do an interview for information with someone who writes for a living and get first hand information. In addition, she should explore internships, or part time/summer jobs in her area of interest, and school activities which involve her interests and enable her to apply her education to her job.

On her goal setting chart, she may wish to go beyond the bachelor degree and include her first job. What would her first job be? She will know of some typical career patterns for writers from her career search. However, Mary is not ready to determine her first job out of college. In her goal setting exercise she will focus on choosing a major. The steps to goal setting are as follows:

1.   Clearly define your goal. Be specific.

2.   Break down your goal into tasks, or your longer term goals into some short term goals. Include your obstacles and solutions.

Overcoming your obstacles may be mini-goals in themselves. Consider and then list all the steps required to achieve your goal.

3.   On a new sheet of paper put your list of tasks, obstacles, solutions and steps into chronological order. Without order, it will be difficult and overwhelming to accomplish your tasks. A step-by-step procedure will help overcome fears, anxiety and simplifies the process.

(Continued)

EXERCISE 18C - Continued

4.Set a date for when you expect these tasks to be completed. Review how much time each step will realistically take to complete and set a completion date for each task. Without a date, it will be easier to procrastinate or brush aside each task. With a date, you give yourself a deadline. You may draw a time line with tasks and dates for visual encouragement. When you have all the steps clearly written to attain your goal, while it may be overwhelming, at least you have some guidelines to follow. We all need guidelines.

There are many other methods of getting organized, and for motivating yourself, and to remind yourself, and to prevent from procrastination. Yearly, monthly and weekly calendars are good reminders. Daily "to do" lists are also useful. Even when organized by nature, write down your goals with deadlines. Make sure these planners, lists or calendars are readily available. Hang up your goals on your refrigerator. Put them on an attractive calendar you like to look at. Keep them by your desk or personal hang-out area, or in your purse, book bag or brief case. This is not something to write down and and then forget about.

These steps and procedures will not guarantee that you follow through on your goal. You will still get discouraged, you will want to give up or do something for fun. To remedy that, I recommend you insert play time into your goal. Taking time out helps us function better. When we are rested, we are more motivated to work. Manage your time well. Don't overwork. Exercise. Don't let tension build up. In addition, include some aspects of your goal while working on getting there. If you want to be a photographer, don't wait until someone hires you to take picutres. Just do it.

And finally, pat yourself on the back every once in awhile for doing a good job. Include in your goal-plan rewards for your accomplishments. Tokens of rewards will encourage you on to the next step.

As with decision making, you need to go back and evaluate how things are going. Are you allowing yourself enough time? Would you like to take a small detour? Has something unforeseen come up? Evaluate and reassess your goals, and consequently your plans. Good luck.

SMITH FAMILY:

SEAN:

Exercise 7 - Values: Financial security, freedom, prestige, power, self-confidence.

Exercise 2 - Childhood Fantasy: Prestigious, high paying job leading others and offering variety and independence.

GOAL: To choose a career path and complete bachelor's degree within three years.

PROBLEMS:
1. Unclear as to what I want for a career and for a major.
2. If I settle for financial security and prestige now (in current work) it may not grow into what I expect and satisfy my life long goals of independence, power, and financial security.

SOLUTIONS:
1. Explore both careers and majors more extensively by talking to people in the various majors I am considering. Find out what alumni from these majors are doing. Interview people (possibly alumni) in the careers I researched. Interview the regional manager of my store.
2. Try out supervisory position. Understand the typical career path of a motivated person in my company and see if it matches my ideal.

STEPS WITH TIME FRAME:
1. December 88 - Take Floor Supervisory position at current job.
2. Fall 88 - Complete general education requirements.
3. February 89 - Interview Regional Manager of The Stereo Shop.
4. Spring 89 - Complete prerequisites for major in business.

(Continued)

5.   Spring 89 - Interview alumnus in each major I am considering.
6.   Summer 89 - Decide to keep job or go to school full-time.
7.   Fall 89 - Declare a major.
8.   Fall 89 through Spring 91 or 92 - Complete requirements for major.
9.   Summer 90 - If not staying in job, do internship.
10.   Fall 90 - Complete writing exit exam to graduate.
11.   Fall 90 - Complete graduation check form.
12.   Fall 90 and Spring 91 - Network, interview for information, prepare resume, and practice interviewing.

MARY:

Exercise 7 - Values: Marriage and family, freedom, aesthetics, health, creativity, peace of mind, wisdom, and travel. Exercise 2 - Childhood Fantasy: Create and be around people who create. Use writing skills.

GOAL: To find a stimulating and interesting major that will provide me with excellent skills and qualifications for a career. The career will involve writing in some capacity.

PROBLEMS:
1. I don't know what the career is.
2. A lot of majors seem interesting.
3. I'm torn between my dream and reality: Will I be a successful writer?
4. I think that the interesting majors may not be the practical ones.

SOLUTIONS:
1. Explore more careers by visiting the career center, attending workshops on different careers, and interviewing someone in each field of interest.
2. I do not have to decide yet. Take courses in all majors that are interesting. Major in one and minor in another. Think more seriously about Comparative Literature major which seems really flexible.
3. I guess I just need to make a go of it. Start writing for school paper, for myself. Enter contests. Take a lot of writing courses and see how good I am.
4. Find out what people end up doing in the "non-practical" majors.

(Continued)

SMITH FAMILY - Continued

STEPS AND TIME FRAME:

1. NOW - Find out what it takes to work on school newspaper.
2. NOW - Find out what other opportunities there are to write, or be published at school.
3. Spring and Fall 89 - Take courses in all majors of interest.
4. Spring and Fall 89 - Take courses that require writing.
5. Spring 89 - Spend one afternoon a month in career center,
6. Spring 89 - Find out what students in my majors of interest are doing through alumni association.
7. Spring 89 - Interview a journalist, magazine editor and a translator.
8. Spring and Fall 89 - Attend any workshops related to writing careers.

MIKE:

Exercise 7 - Values: Marriage and family, self-confidence, knowledge, freedom, altruism, prestige . Exercise 2 - Childhood Fantasy: To work outdoors. Observe animals.

GOAL: To become more involved with my first career choice by joining ecologically-minded groups, exploring graduate programs in Biology and eventually entering such a program.

PROBLEMS:
1. Not enough time to go to school and work full-time.
2. Anne is also in school and is not working.
3. How can I stay in current career and blatantly pursue another?
4. There may be financial hazards with four of us in college and one pay check.
5. I may not be able to academically cut it.
6. I'm afraid I may like it too much and not be able to go as far as I want.

SOLUTIONS:
1. Will have to change life-style in terms of leisure time and priorities by cutting out golf on weekends, and structuring my time during week nights. Pursue crazy idea of job sharing. Investigate consulting opportunities.
2. I guess the hazard here is that Anne is not working. I don't want to discourage her. We will have to work out a suitable compromise so that we are both happy. For instance, Anne could work part-time.
3. This is a problem because I still am unsure. Once I know it's not so crazy, it won't be a problem. I haven't really decided on changing careers, I'm merely returning to school.

(Continued)

4. Again, Anne could start working. I could put off my plans until Anne has a job and at least Sean is out of school. We could cut down on expenses. The kids could help with their expenses.
5. Take some refresher courses before I apply.
6. Not worry about it.

STEPS AND TIME FRAME:

1. December 88 - Thoroughly discuss plans with family.

2. January 88 - Join Sierra Club, National Audubon Society and National Wildlife Federation.

3. 1/89 - 4/89 - Investigate Ph.D programs in Biology with options for master's degrees.

4. 1/89 - 4/89 - Find another way to get involved during my free time, for instance, running a nature tour, volunteering at a zoo.

5. 1/89 - 6/89 - Investigate consulting opportunities in my current field.

6. 1989 - Take two or three refresher courses in my field.

7. Summer 1989 - Evaluate and decide whether I want to pursue graduate school.

8. August 1989 - Take GRE.

9. November 1989 - Apply to graduate program.

10. 1989 - Review budget and discuss financial plans with Anne. See feasibility for me to eventually pursue school full-time and work part- time.

(Continued)

SMITH FAMILY - Continued

11.   Summer 89 - Investigate opportunities for job sharing at work.

12.   Fall 1990 - Begin master's program in Zoology on a part-time basis.

13.   End of Fall 90 - Evaluate.

ANNE:

Exercise 7 - Values: Marriage and family, financial security, self-confidence, work I love, and travel.

Exercise 2 - Chilhood Fantasy: Be in beautiful old homes.

GOAL: To open my own antique business.

PROBLEMS:
1. I'm scared. I lack self-confidence. I fear failure.
2. We don't have the money for me to begin a business.
3. I don't have all the know how of running a business.
4. I'd like a partner, but am not sure how to find someone I trust.
5. I'm not sure I'll have the energy, confidence and enthusiasm it takes.
6. I'm not sure that Mike will really be able to handle being married to not only a working women, but a business woman, especially because he is going through a little bit of a mid-life crisis. I'm mostly concerned that he won't like all the traveling I'll be doing without him!
7. Somewhat concerned about leaving children.

SOLUTIONS:
1. Visualize myself successful. Read and say affirmations. Share my ideas with people who are supportive. Make sure that my husband is supportive.
2. This is tough. I could take out a loan. I could dip into our retirement money. I could work a job that pays well and save for several years (postpone my plans), we could sell the house and live frugally (I don't like that idea). I could find a partner with the money.

(Continued)

SMITH FAMILY - Continued

3.   Take classes on running a small business. Land a job where I would have management responsibilities and could quickly learn what I don't know.

4.   I could easily find a financial partner amongst our friends. I know some people in the business, but not many. Once I am working I may meet others. Maybe when Sean matures a little, he would be interested.

5.   I will see as I slowly work my way into it by working and schooling.

6.   We will have to sit down and talk about our plans and dreams. I will have to be sensitive to his dreams. I will have to become more assertive about my dreams. Learn to cope with adjustments.

7.   By the time I'm ready, my kids will be on their own.

PART THREE

DYNAMICS OF JOB SEARCH

CHAPTER XII:

DYNAMICS OF JOB SEARCH

RESUME

Just like the word *"examination,"* *"writing"* is a word that creates a fearful reaction with most students. People strongly dislike writing resumes, and will spend a great deal of money to hire others to do it for them. Aside from the dislike for writing, I believe the avoidance of writing resumes comes from two sources: We are insecure about our skills and qualifications. We don't want to bother with the research and work that goes into writing a resume.

You have spent a great deal of time on self-awareness by analyzing your values, personality, interests, and skills. The resume is the end result of this introspective search.

If you have closely followed the suggested assignments in this book, you will be nearer to the completion of your resume than you may realize. From the

Experience List and Skills Category exercises you will have a list of personal, technical and functional skills. You will need this list to write your resume.

What is a resume? It is a summary of your skills and qualifications geared toward a job objective. The purpose of a resume is to obtain an interview. There are two basic types of resumes: chronological and functional.

CHRONOLOGICAL

The most common type is the chronological resume, which lists your skills and qualifications under headings of your past places of employment in reverse chronological order. You will list where and when you have worked, your job title and duties for that particular position. This resume is most useful when you have worked for one or only a few companies in which you have performed the same kind of work, or when you have consistently been promoted in your company. If you have this type of work history and are planning to continue in the same field, a chronological resume is the type you should use.

FUNCTIONAL

On a functional resume your skills and qualifications are listed under broad categories of functional/transferable skills, as discussed in the chapter on skills. The functional resume is used by individuals with a limited work history, or those with employment gaps, or by career changers. The purpose of a functional resume is to summarize the skills you have acquired from past employment, schooling or other activities, and gear them toward a particular job target. The job target is the field you are planning to enter, or a specific job you may be seeking. The target may be as general as: A position in which I may utilize my communication and organizational skills. Or it may be specific, such as: To obtain a counseling position working with children who have been abused. It will be easier to write your resume toward a specific goal because you need only to list those skills that are necessary for the job, leaving out the superfluous and unrelated. If you are applying for jobs in different fields, write a resume for each field. There are three variations of functional resumes: the basic functional, the combination, and the capability functional.

The basic functional resume contains skills organized in broad categories. You do not include previous places of employment.

The combination resume contains your categories of skills and under a separate heading your work history. When listing your history, do not include job duties, since these have already been incorporated in the skills section on the resume. Only list the name (and address if you choose) of the place of employment, your job title(s), and dates employed (optional). If you have done volunteer work, include the skills used under your skill categories and the job title under your work history indicating that you were a volunteer.

The third type of functional resume not only includes skills and a brief work history, but your capabilities.* Skills are assessed in three ways: achievement, or what you have accomplished, ability, or what you are now able to do, and aptitude, or what you predict you can achieve. The capabilities portion of your resume will show the employer what you are capable of performing based on your past accomplishments.

Capabilities are not synonymous to skills. They may not have been performed in a job setting, but are inferred from both life and work experiences. For instance, in your previous job as a sales clerk you increased sales in your department by twenty-five percent. Most of this increase has been a result of your own sales, but you have also encouraged other employees to increase their sales. You have made several suggestions on the displaying of products, and you have taken on some of the manager's duties when she was away. You also started a child care co- op with your friends and neighbors, and even after the co-op was well under way, the members came to you to solve problems. Based on these experiences you could include as a capability that you have leadership qualities, the ability to encourage others to increase their sales, and can handle the shop while management is out.

Sometimes you may not be clear as to whether a capability is a skill, or an aptitude. The rule of thumb is that a capability is something you know you can do but it is not in your job description, or you have not performed on a job. You may want to combine capabilities and accomplishments under one heading as Anne did on her resume under "Qualifications." There is no set rule on how to describe your capabilities, qualifications, accomplishments and skills. The point is to emphasize the skills that are most important for your job objective, as well as stressing your best skills.

---

*Build a Resume," *BUSINESS WEEK CAREERS*. Ann Arbor: McGraw Hill Publication, June 1988, pp 38-47

In order to write any type of functional resume, you must first categorize your skills under major headings. Table 8 - Skills List has categories of functional skills arranged into data, people, thing and idea headings, and listed from most difficult to least difficult within each category. These are the same skill categories as described in the *DICTIONARY OF OCCUPATIONAL TITLES*. The samples are not meant to constrain or prevent you from determining your own skill categories.

The purpose of classifying your skills is threefold: First, analyzing your experiences and skills leads to self-understanding. It also teaches your brain-computer to be organized. Second, you will save the hundred dollars it costs to have someone do this for you. With your skills analyzed and classified you have just about written your resume. It is a wonderful preparation exercise not only for resume-writing, but also for interviewing. Preparing your resume is like studying for a test; the test being your interview. Third, by identifying and categorizing your skills you will come to realize that you have more skills and qualifications than you originally thought. This exercise may increase your self-confidence.

EXERCISE 19 - RESUME PREPARATION

There are four steps in skills analysis: Identifying skills necessary for the job; identifying the skills you have for the job; identifying your aptitude for the job (capabilities); organizing your skills in a presentable manner.

Step 1: From job announcements, interviews for information, job descriptions, or basic career research, make a list of technical, personal and transferable skills necessary for your job objective. Organize these skills into broad categories (use Table 8 - Skills List if necessary).

Step 2: Compare the skills from step 1 with those from Exercise 10 - Skill Categories to evaluate which skills you already have performed competently.

Step 3: Consider how you may have the potential to perform the remaining skills so you can show your aptitude (or capabilities) on your resume. A good interviewer may be able to predict your aptitude, but the purpose of a resume is to get an interview; tell them your predictions so you will get the interview.

Step 4A: Classify your skills (those underlined) into broad categories that are necessary for the job objective. These categories serve a basic function, and have been repeated (transferred) in different jobs and activities. For instance, in counseling, you build rapport, listen actively, make suggestions, guide, direct, inform, and question. The skills are part of one function which could be called interpersonal communication. As a clerk working with the public, you provide information, refer people to other offices/agencies, question, probe to understand peoples' questions, and explain procedures or forms. And as a receptionist you provide information, refer to appropriate offices or personnel, and ask and answer questions. In all three jobs you are using communication skills, and in each job speaking and listening is a major function of the job. By using the skills in different contexts, you have transferred them from one job to the next.

(Continued)

EXERCISE 19 - Continued

On a resume, you list your skills and experiences under major headings as shown on the Smith Family resume samples. Typical headings are: organizing, supervising communicating, writing, planning, evaluating, researching and teaching. (Refer to the *Skills List* in Table 8) The headings will depend on the job you are seeking. For a service profession skill headings would include nurturing and attending, communication, organization or administrative, and possibly a technical category pertaining to the particular field. As you may have noticed, all of the skills listed above are functional.

When writing a resume for a technical job, most of your skills will be specific to a job and will fall under major headings of technical skills. For instance, a Graphic Artist may have the following technical categories: Design, Layout, Rendering and Photography. She may then include some transferable skills such as, customer relations, and shop management.

Some jobs include a series of steps and procedures. For instance, in sales, you approach the customer, question his needs, suggest a product, help him decide, persuade him to buy it and close the deal. All of these skills could fall under a general category of Salesmanship. Notice that some of the skills listed under salesmanship are also communication skills. You will find that many of your skills fall into several categories. Decide which categories best describe your skills and are most appropriate for your job objective.

Step 4B. The last part of this step is to rank your skills from most difficult to the least difficult, with number one being the most difficult and up to least difficult.

For example, under the heading of CLERICAL are: scheduling travel arrangements (2), typing letters and memorandums on typewriter (4), filing (5) and duplicating (6), operating computer using Symphony spread sheets (1), and typing or word processing (3). You will also rank the major headings in order of difficulty or by relevance to your job objective. For a sales office manager position list your major categories in the following manner: management, organization, administrative. Or for a clerical position requiring heavy computer experience put: computer, organization, clerical.

(Continued)

EXERCISE 19 - Continued

Step 5. You will not list all of your skills on your resume. Only use the skills that most appropriately describe your qualifications for the job you are seeking. You may want to highlight or emphasize certain skills by putting them under the capabilities or qualification category as in a newspaper caption. You can expand on those skills further down the page in the experience section. Draw as much as you can from all your life experiences .

TABLE 8 - SKILLS LIST*

DATA & IDEAS:

Synthesize:
Creating art, music, crafts, writing, acting, etc.
Designing a concept for remodeling the kitchen.
Explaining abstract idea to young person.

Other words or phrases:
Problem-solve, imagine, visualize, perceive, invent, combine, compose, reason, unify, conceive.

Coordinate:
Initiate babysitting co-op.
Organize a ski trip.
Review and evaluate how you did on an interview.

Other words or phrases:
Evaluate, decide, make policy, trouble-shoot, develop, set goal, adjust, equalize, plan, forecast, project, schedule, anticipate, assign, consolidate, cooperate, prepare, schedule, review, demonstrate.

Analyze:
Identify ingredients in a food item.
Interpret complicated instructions or diagrams.
Analyze costs for vacation trip.

Other words or phrases:
Diagnose, separate, understand, edit, improve, break down, classify, differentiate, discriminate, discuss, dissect, reason, examine, inquire, research, investigate, evaluate, arrange, formulate, assess, compare, inspect, judge, measure, review, select, interpret.

(Continued)

Dictionary of Occupational Titles, U.S. Department of Labor, 1977

TABLE 8 - SKILLS LIST- Continued

Compile:
Classify records (music) by style or groups.
Follow specific procedures as in balancing checkbook.
Remember customer names.

Other words or phrases: Assemble, gather, collect, accumulate, conglomerate, aggregate, combine, compare, screen, inspect, classify, layout, accurate, measure, review, select.

Compute:
Compute area of room, or yard.
Calculate monthly output for bills.

Other words or phrases:
Add, measure, sum, total, balance, estimate, figure, decipher, gauge, quantify, estimate, appraise, evaluate, assay, weigh, reason, survey.

Copy:
Copy class notes from a friend.
Rewrite assignment for neatness.
Take inventory of moving items.

Other words or phrases:
Diagram, reproduce, substitute, duplicate, repeat, remake, replicate, write.

Compare:
Compare brand items in the store.
File papers alphabetically or numerically.
Match size of bolts to screws.

Other words and phrases:
Observe, examine, inspect, survey, match, proofread, classify, retrieve, approximate, correspond, parallel, simulate.

(Continued)

TABLE 8 - SKILLS LIST - Continued

PEOPLE

Mentor:
Support friend who is seriously troubled.
Encourage teammate to keep trying.
Make friend with new neighbor/schoolmate.

Other words or phrases:
Comfort, counsel, heal, develop rapport, advise, evaluate, motivate, teach, rehabilitate, facilitate.

Negotiate:
Mediate dispute between children.
Argue for a different approach.
Promote new product.

Other words or phrases:
Bargain, discuss, contract, recruit, represent, promote, persevere, confront, collaborate, compromise, discuss options, interpret, recommend, select, submit.

Instruct:
Teach children rules to a game.
As team captain, lead team members.
Train new employee.

Other words or phrases:
Coach, advise, direct, inform, command, counsel, recommend, suggest, advocate, propose, submit, guide, prescribe, confer, consult, enlighten, communicate, disclose, report, educate, show, demonstrate, motivate, support, encourage, catechize.

Supervise:
Delegate household duties to family members.
Oversee trainee to insure that work is correctly completed.
Assign housekeeper/gardener specific tasks.

(Continued)

TABLE 8 - SKILLS LIST - Continued

Other words or phrases:
Initiate, lead, motivate, review, organize, direct, begin, head, influence, coordinate personnel, pioneer, precede, impel, stimulate, commission, communicate, establish priority, evaluate, revise, train, recruit, interview, organize, govern.

Divert:
Demonstrate how to use ski equipment.
Compose jingle for birthday card.

Other words or phrases:
Write, act, sing, direct play, play instrument, play sports, public speaking, model, amuse, entertain, beguile, enliven, delight.

Persuade:
Convince someone to change their mind about an idea.
Initiate a conversation with a shy person.
Advertise the sale of your car.

Other words or phrases:
Deal, sell, develop rapport, relate, promote, convert, convince, induce, influence, collaborate, compromise, discuss, mediate, recommend, select options, submit ideas.

Speak/Signal:
Describe problem of a defective purchase over the telephone.
Signal to children to stay away from area in play yard.
Communicate message to customer.

Other words or phrases:
Express, order, define, gesture, interpersonal communication, non-verbal behavior, impart, converse, inform, give, transfer, address, affirm, remark, hint, sign.

(Continued)

TABLE 8 - SKILLS LIST - Continued

Serve:
Care for family pet.
Offer assistance to customer.
Decorate for a party.

Other words or phrases: Help, give, tend, aid, benefit, support, relief, comfort, service, expedite, render, cater, attend.

THINGS:

Precision Work:
Shape/sculpture clay into figure.
Design floor plans for house.
Type a form letter.

Other words or phrases:
Shape, draft, illustrate, draw, play a musical instrument, layout, paste-up, finger dexterity, hand-eye coordination, use precision tools.

Operate/Control:
Operate a computer, cash register, sewing machine, electric sander, etc.

Other words or phrases:
Function, run, use, play, handle, manipulate, maneuver, drive, steer, guide, utilize.

Drive/Operate:
Drive any vehicle or heavy equipment.

Other words or phrases:
Run, use handle, manipulate, maneuver, steer, utilize, operate, pilot, helm, steer, navigate, thrust.

(Continued)

TABLE 8 - SKILLS LIST - Continued

Manipulate:
Construct model airplane.
Assemble dress with sewing machine.
Cultivate vegetable garden.

Other words or phrases:
Build, repair, grow, form, produce, fabricate, put together, prepare, mold, raise, devise, concoct, piece together, restore, fix, recondition, overhaul, furbish, touch up, vamp, polish, spruce up, farm, raise, rear.

Handle:
Lift, pull, balance or push a tool, instrument or machine.

Other words or phrases:
Elevate, raise, transport, deflect, extract, restrain, row, hasten, propel, shove, offset, stabilize, retrieve.

SOME GENERAL RULES FOR RESUMES:

1. One page for every ten years of employment experience. Be concise. Work with the format of your resume so that is fits onto one page. Do not leave the last portion of your resume on a separate page. Rewrite so that it will fit on one page.

2. Use a clear, neat, consistent and attractive layout. Remember, your resume is an extension of you and the only thing the employer has to evaluate you. Be sure you have no typing, grammatical or spelling errors. Use one tense, preferably the present tense. Have someone else proof your resume. If you do not type well, have someone type it for you, or have it printed. It is a worthy investment.

3. Start sentences with action verbs and use skill words and use the language of the industry.

4. Highlight your accomplishments. For example, "Established retail contacts, resulting in a 10% increased product distribution," or "Received literary prize for short story."

5. Make strong statements. Do not include superfluous or non-pertinent information. Keep you sentences short and to the point.

6. List employment and education in reverse chronological order.

7. List your skills, accomplishments and capabilities with the highest level first. Interviewers and personnel employees read hundreds, or even thousands of resumes. The items you want them to see should be at the top of the resume and at the top of each section of the resume.

8. *Do not* list age, sex, maritial status, height, weight and other personal descriptions, unless they are required for the job.

9. *Do not* list salary history, reasons for termination and unemployment.

RESUME PREPARATION

THE FORMAT FOR RESUMES IS AS FOLLOWS:

1. Centered or at one side is your name, address and phone number(s) where you can be reached.

2. Employment objective: Type of position, and/or general field you are searching.

3. Capabilities: A list of skills for which you have an aptitude. They should be skills desirable for your job objective.

4. Education: If you have recently finished college, are still attending college, or your college degree will be a major factor in your acquiring a position, list your education before your work experience or qualifications. List any awards or scholarships received. List your grade point average only when it is impressive (above a 3.0). When still attending college or high school, indicate your expected graduation date. Do not list education fourth if any of the following descriptions fit: You have a very strong work history, or skills that are more impressive than your education; your education is not relevant to the job; or it has been several years since you have completed your education.

5. Experience, skills or qualifications (whichever title you use) are listed before education when education is less impressive, or after education when your education is more impressive. When writing a chronological resume, you would list your work history instead of skills and qualifications by classifications (see Mike's resume). When writing a functional resume, you will list your skills under the heading of EMPLOYMENT EXPERIENCE or QUALIFICATIONS. If you choose, you may include a work history.

6. List special activities or skills, or interests that may help you get the job.

7. REFERENCES AVAILABLE UPON REQUEST. You will type a separate page with references. Depending on the needs of the employer, you may list personal or professional (employment related) references, or a combination of both. Three to five references are standard. List their names, titles (when appropriate), place of employment (when appropriate), address and phone number where they can be reached.

EXERCISE 20 - RESUME

1. Make a list of the places you have worked. Include supervisor's name, company, address, phone number, titles and dates of employment. Also include any type of volunteer work.

2. Make a list of schools you have attended, courses relevant to your job goal, and extra-curricular activities relevant to your job goal.

3. Organize your resume using the above information and Exercise 19 - Resume Preparation.

SMITH FAMILY

Exercise 19 - Resume Preparation

Exercise 20 - The Resume

ANNE:

Steps 1 and 2. **Technical**: Extensive knowledge of furniture styles, historic periods and furniture values. Knowledge of woods, construction and refinishing procedures. Business contacts and referral sources. Bookkeeping and accounting procedures. **Transferable**: Organize people and tasks. Match tasks to appropriate staff. Identify and handle wide range of customer needs. Answer questions and obtain resources to insure customer satisfaction. Interact with customers, wholesalers, buyers, refinishing personnel, and movers. Attractively arrange furniture and other items. Ability to lift heavy objects.
Personal: Attentive, organized, imaginative, resourceful, assertive, confident, directive.

Step 3. **Bookkeeping and accounting procedures** — Know basic procedures from household budgeting, and fund-raising experiences. Can learn through college course.

Interact with customers, wholesalers, etc. — Directed several fund-raising programs in which I was responsible for contacting and persuading members of the community to donate various items (from one dollar to several thousand); made mailing lists, scouted for sources. Have also acquired several exotic pieces of furniture through my network of resources, and by traveling to Europe, Asia and the East Coast.

Identify and handle wide range of customer needs, answer questions, insure satisfaction — Sold items at fund-raisers. Have located particular pieces for friends and relatives. Arrange and lift furniture — Usually lift furniture at home. Arrange furniture at home and for friends.

(Continued)

SMITH FAMILY - Continued

Step 4. **Negotiating**: Promote fundraising plan, and activities to community and education board. Persuade local businesses to donate items or services. Representing P.T.A. and Mothers Against Drugs. Recruiting mothers to volunteer. Negotiate for best price when buying or selling.

Coordinating: Organize committees for particular projects. Initiate several fund-raising projects. Trouble-shoot between parents, and volunteers. Set financial goals for fund-raising projects. Organize schedules for volunteers, car pools, fund-raising events, children's summer activities, and vacation itinerary.

Supervising: Assign volunteers tasks which appropriately fit their abilities. Train and delegate children in household or homework tasks, and volunteers in their duties. Evaluate their work and suggest changes for improvement. Motivate volunteers to do a good job.

Administration: Design procedures for acquiring goods. Inventory and budgeting of items. Handle all bookkeeping for fund-raisers. Compile mailing list for several fund-raisers.

Anne will also use a functional resume highlighting her capabilities (qualifications) since she has been unemployed for several years, and will be drawing most of her experiences as a volunteer work and homemaker.

(Continued)

Anne Marie Smith
3736 Memory Lane
San Joaquin, CA 92636
(987) 654-3210

OBJECTIVE:
A growth oriented sales-position in the antique business with management potential.

QUALIFICATIONS:
Extensive knowledge of antique history, pricing, and restoration. Negotiate best price when buying and selling. Trouble-shoot problems with customers, workers, and management. Initiate projects to encourage sales. Set and achieve financial goal of $50,000. Direct and motivate employees.

EXPERIENCE. Negotiating: Promote fund-raising plan to community and education board. Persuade local businesses to donate items or services. Recruit volunteers for various positions. **Coordinating**: Initiate several fund-raising projects. Organize committees, make schedules for volunteers, and fund-raising events. Arrange Asian and European travel itineraries. **Supervising**: Assign volunteers tasks which appropriately fit their abilities. Train and delegate volunteers. Evaluate work and suggest changes for improvement. Motivate others to do a good job. **Administration**: Design procedures for acquiring goods and services from local businesses. Inventory and budgeting of items. Handle all bookkeeping for fund-raisers. Compile mailing list for several fund-raisers.

- Treasurer and Secretary, Mothers Against Drugs, 1986-87
- President, San Joaquin Historical Society, 1987
- President, Parent Teacher Association, 1984-85
- Treasurer, Parent Teacher Association, 1983-84
- Member, Antiques Guild, 1982-89
- San Joaquin Community Library, Clerk, 1982-1984

EDUCATION
Candidate for Associate of Arts Degree in Business, 1991 Valley Community College
San Joaquin University, Liberal Arts Major, 1968-70

TRAVEL:
Extensive travel experience throughout the U.S.A., Asia, Europe.

REFERENCES AVAILABLE UPON REQUEST

MARY:

Steps 1 and 2. **Technical**: knowledgeable of school, local and world events; typing (60 wpm); express facts and opinions clearly and succinctly.
Functional: locate sources; gather information; present different points of view; prepare and write stories.
Personal: accurate, objective, curious, persistent, initiative, resourceful, accurate memory.

Step 3. **Knowledge** of school, local and world events — I learn about things that interest me. Thus, as a journalist, I would need to be knowledgeable of my subject area. It might be a good idea, however, to start reading more newspapers (school and local paper).

Present different points of view and objectivity — I'm not always objective. Am learning from courses to be more critical, objective, and see other points of view, and how to present these from Composition course. **Interview people** — I'm not really bold, and a little shy. This is something I could overcome with practice. I did talk with several of the students who visited our school from different places for the Model U.N. I also approach customers at the store, and find out what they need. **Accurate memory** — I do forget details. However, the Learning Center at school has a workshop on memory that I will attend. It would be better for me to get a position as a movie or book critic, but I know I'd have to prove myself first.

Step 4. **Research Skills:** Locate sources for information on subject, review background information, analyze importance of information and summarize for piece. **Writing Skills**: First place in school literary contest. Write objectively (impartial) and accurately for paper on apartheid; write creative fiction pieces for school literary magazine. Edit other's work. Good grammar and usage.

(Continued)

SMITH FAMILY - Continued

Interpersonal Communication: Approach individuals, appropriately phrase questions to acquire necessary information, listen carefully for details, observe non verbal behavior, and show genuine interest to encourage interviewee.

Publication: Organize and plan magazine layout and paste-up, including illustrative pieces, copy and proofreading, typing (50 wpm) and word processing (65 wpm).

SAMPLE OF CAPABILITIES RESUME

Since Mary has limited work experience, she will write a functional resume to enhance her qualifications with courses taken, and other work/life experiences. She will indicate her aptitude by including her capabilities.

Mary L. Smith
3736 Memory Lane
San Joaquin, CA 92636
(987) 654-3210

OBJECTIVE:
Position as a general assignment reporter or copy editor.

EDUCATION:
Attending California University
Diploma from Saddleback High School, June 1988
Saddleback Literary Prize, 1988
Grade Point Average: 3.4.

CAPABILITIES:
Spot a good story. Persist for information. Work well under deadlines and pressure.
Take initiative in a variety of situations. Innovative in finding sources of information

EXPERIENCE:

WRITING: Write creative fiction pieces for school literary magazine. Produce impartial and accurate pieces for Cultural Awareness project. Write in depth critical term papers.

PUBLICATION: Design magazine layout. Execute paste-up, copy editing and proofreading. Utilize Wordstar wordprocessing software (65 wpm).

RESEARCH: Locate sources for data or knowledge on subject. Review background information. Analyze and summarize gathered facts.

INTERPERSONAL COMMUNICATION: Effectively approach and address individuals. Appropriately phrase questions to acquire information. Actively listen for details. Carefully observe non-verbal behavior. Genuinely show interest to encourage interviewee.

HISTORY: Sales Clerk, Fashion Place, June 89 - present
Editor, *WORDS*, 1988

REFERENCES AVAILABLE UPON REQUEST

SMITH FAMILY

SEAN:

Steps 1 and 2. **Functional**: Plan, schedule, and supervise day-to-day work of employees. Train employees. Assist in hiring of new employees. Solve disputes between employees. Solve customer problems. Sell merchandise. Balance register. Handle sales transactions. Communicate with vendors. Handle problems with vendors.

Technical: Knowledge of stereo and electronic components. Basic bookkeeping. Keep record of inventory and sales.

Personal: Extroverted, persuasive, leadership, organized, think-on-feet, fair, diplomatic.

Step 3. **Plan and schedule work** — plan and schedule my own work, school and free time. Planned and organized school dances. In charge of music and public address system. Also planned school and personal (overnight) ski outings.

Assist in hiring of new employees — Recommended responsible friend for job.

Handle problems with vendors — Have handled problems with coworkers, and customers. Good communication and persuasive skills I see as transferable.

Bookkeeping — Can learn on the job.

Step 4. **Customer Service**: Analyze and approach customer, influence their decisions, handle exchanges and customer problems, ring up purchases.

Administrative: Open and close (balance) registers, interact with vendors, plan and organize school events and outings, assist in hiring new employees, train and supervise new employees. Coordinate stockroom and shop to meet selling and restocking needs.

Electronics Knowledge: Familiar with approximately fifty brand names and their advantages, disadvantages and inner workings. Usually can identify problem and suggest solution for non-working components from customer description. Keep abreast of new models and inventions.

(Continued)

SAMPLE OF FUNCTIONAL RESUME

Sean will write a functional resume, including his capabilities, because he is seeking advancement and wants to convince the employers that he has the aptitude for the promotion.

Sean Michael Smith
3736 Memory Lane
San Joaquin, CA 92636
(987) 654-3210

OBJECTIVE:
Seek an entry-level, growth oriented management position in a stereo and high
fidelity shop.

EDUCATION:
Attending California University; Major: Business
Diploma, Saddleback High School, 1987

CAPABILITIES:
Forecast future market trends by examining and analyzing customer
preferences and buying habits.
Inspire a spirit of teamwork among co-workers.
Encourage customer return by insuring product satisfaction.
Develop channels of communication with management, vendors and customers.

EXPERIENCE:

CUSTOMER SERVICE : Sell stereo equipment at $12,000 per month, leading
the part-time staff for three quarters. Solve customer problems and grievances.
ADMINISTRATIVE: Maintain control of administrative duties while
management is unavailable. Assist in hiring, training and supervising of new
employees. Communicate with vendors regarding orders. Open and close
(balance) registers. Coordinate stockroom and shop to meet selling and
restocking needs.
EXPERTISE: Familiar with fifty brand names, including advantages,
disadvantages and inner workings. Identify problems and suggest solution for
non-working components from customer description. Keep abreast of new
models and engineering.

EMPLOYMENT : December 1987 - present The Stereo Place, Salesman.
June 1986 - August 1987 Hamburgers Are US, Counter Clerk.

AFFILIATIONS: Water Polo Team Captain, 1986-1987; Entertainment
Committee Chair, 1987; Ski Club, 1986-1987; Junior Class Student Government
Rep, 1986.

REFERENCES AVAILABLE UPON REQUEST

Smith Family - Continued

SAMPLE OF CHRONOLOGICAL RESUME

Mike has consistent and comprehensive experience in one field, has had few employment changes and has been promoted over the years.

Michael D. Smith
3736 Memory Lane
San Joaquin, CA 92636
(987) 654-3210 (home) (987) 654-0123 (work)

OBJECTIVE: Position as a Senior Planner

QUALIFICATIONS:

- Supervise staff of sixteen
- Extensive research and analysis experience
- Develop and coordinate planning activities
- Communicate and coordinate with governing agencies

EXPERIENCE:

Planning Division City of San Joaquin 2300 Main Street San Joaquin, CA 94638

April 1976 - June 1984: **Associate Planner:** Organize and conduct research studies utilizing various sources of information; compose complete reports of research findings; make analysis and recommendations based on research findings; work effectively with general public and community agencies concerning matters of land uses related to planning functions; interpret and apply laws to planning projects; and supervise and coordinate work of others.

January 1972 - March 1976: **Assistant Planner:** Assist in preparation of planning studies, reports, plans, and projects; explain to public the planning program, policies, ordinances and regulations; make field investigations; prepare displays and exhibits for public presentation.

January 1971 - December 1972: **Planning Aide:** Assist planning staff with compiling data and tabulations. Produce statistical information for reports. Answer inquiries from public regarding zoning, population estimates and general plans.

EDUCATION:

Certificate in Planning and Public Policy, 1975 San Joaquin University
Bachelor of Science in Biology, 1970 California University

AFFILIATIONS: Member of California Institute of Planners

REFERENCES AVAILABLE UPON REQUEST

COVER LETTER

The purpose of a cover letter is to highlight the important aspects of your resume. It is a letter of introduction. The same rules regarding spelling and neatness that apply to the resume apply to the cover letter.

Before you write your cover letter, you must do some basic investigation. Find out the name of your potential boss, or the person who is hiring, and address the cover letter to that person. If you do not have a name or a contact, your resume will go to personnel — along with several hundred others. By sending your resume to the person hiring, you may have a better chance that your particular qualifications are noticed by the person who counts.

It's important to know something about the company to which you are applying. In your cover letter include the reasons you want to work with that particular firm or agency. Be able to recite specific skills you have that are necessary for the job. Think of your accomplishments, successes, special skills and talents, or positive aspects of your personality. Think of what you can *contribute to* the company, not what they can contribute to your career goals. Use words such as "offer," "contribute," and "mutually rewarding." A cover letter should be short and to the point. You will indicate in your cover letter:

1) How you learned about the position (use a name if you have one).

2) Why you are interested in the position/firm.

3) What particular skills, assets you have to offer the firm.

4) What is unique about you?

Show enthusiasm and interest in the position and in the firm.

BASIC HINTS:

Be positive and confident. Ask for an interview. Close the deal by telling them you will call for an interview at such and such time. Accent the positive and eliminate the negative. Use an attention getting introduction. Be sure you have correct headings, titles, and addressees. Use quality paper in ivory, white or grey. Any quality bond paper is fine.

Example: Because my career includes five years experience working with diverse populations in depressed environments, I feel I can make a significant contribution to your organization. I have worked with all age groups and have established mutually rewarding relationships. I have been especially successful with delinquent young people.

EXERCISE 21 - COVER LETTER

Write a cover letter, using this example as a form:

Sean Michael Smith
3736 Memory Lane
San Joaquin, CA 92636 (987) 654-3210

November 26, 1990

Mr. Gerald Middleton, Regional Manager
The Stereo Place
1734 Grand Avenue
San Joaquin, CA 92636

Dear Mr. Middleton,

David O'Connell encouraged me to apply for the Assistant Manager position at the shop in San Joaquin. Enclosed you will find a copy of my resume.

In my first year at the Stereo Place I increased overall sales by twenty percent, and I have been the leading part-time sales person for the last year and a half. I not only have excellent customer relations, I am recognized by my co-workers as a leader. I have frequently taken on additional responsibilities to help current management, especially during the busy cycles. As you can see on my resume, I am attending California University pursuing a degree in business. After acquiring my degree I intend to advance into a marketing position with the shop.

I will be contacting you about an interview at the end of this week. Or, you may call me at (987) 654-3210. I look forward to meeting with you.

Sincerely,

Sean Michael Smith

Anna Marie Smith
3736 Memory Lane
San Joaquin, CA 92636
(987) 654-3210

December 12, 1990

Ms. Jaime Albeno
Second Time Around
302 Spring Street
San Joaquin, CA 92636

Dear Ms. Albeno:

As per our telephone conversation, enclosed is a copy of my resume. I am very interested in the management position at your store. I know and have bought several pieces from your former manager, Cathrine Neuwman.

Through my seven years experience buying and selling with your store, I am aware of your style and preferences. It would be rewarding to work in your shop because of the quality of your collection and our common interest in Chinese workmanship. I have been a collector for seven years, and a member of the Guild for five years. I have traveled extensively and have several contacts in Europe and Asia. In addition, I have several years experience as a fund-raiser, and therefore, am comfortable with administration and public relations.

I look forward to the opportunity to speak with you again. I will call you in two weeks after returning from my trip.

Sincerely,

Anna Marie Smith

ACTIVE SEARCH

Whether you are looking your first career position, or are making a career transition, you will want to be sure that you land the the perfect job. Finding a job takes forethought, investigation and persistence. There are two ways to approach job search: passively and actively. By passive, I mean responding to ads or employers inquiries, or by allowing the employer to take the initiative. By active, I mean approaching perspective employers whether or not they have an ad for an opening, or by your taking the initiative. When approaching the employer before he has advertised a position, you are not competing with all the others responding to an ad, and you are showing your enthusiasm, confidence and resourcefulness.

Your active research will include reading materials about companies and particular fields, and communicating with friends and acquaintances about your field of interest. Subscribe to and read trade publications, and professional journals. Investigate materials available at libraries, government agencies, educational institutions. (See Table 9) Know what is happening in your field. Trade publications also advertise jobs.

Networking is an excellent method for finding a job. Tell everyone, including, friends, acquaintances, grocer, hairdresser, mechanic, doctor, neighbor, family, and teachers, that you are seeking employment. Joining professional organizations increases your network of contacts and keeps you informed.

After acquiring contacts and researching firms of interest, interview the companies to explore whether you would like to work for them. It is better to research your field, or different companies before you begin to apply. When YOU are the interviewee, YOU will be more anxious and pressured to impress. When you are identifying which companies are for you, they are on the spot. If you have a name, make an appointment with that individual. If you do not have a name, get the name. Find the department that matches your job objective, and make an appointment with the head of that department. Tell him you are exploring companies to find the one that best matches your skills and interests. If you get a "we're not hiring," or "call personnel," do not feel defeated. Ask if you may send a resume, or whether they may need someone at a later date. The worst they can tell you is "no." Most likely, they will be interested in someone who is actively seeking employment, taking initiative, assertive enough to know what they want and confident enough to know what they have to offer.

If you are attending college, begin your job search during the last two years of school by networking and interviewing for information. Interning while still at school serves as an excellent source for contacts and provides experience in your field of interest. These efforts serve a dual purpose: making contacts and exploring interests. By mid-senior year, you should have several contacts, have written a resume and have practiced for your interviews. By your last semester, you are well on your way to actively seeking employment. You certainly may include passive methods, such as responding to ads, on campus interviews, and following leads through acquaintances.

Some basic tools and hints for your job search are:

1.   Keep a notebook. In your notebook keep the names of companies, contact persons, any information on either; dates of when you have either telephoned or written to these people and dates for call backs.

2.   Keep a calendar for appointments, important dates and other events.

3.   Make to do lists and priority lists.

INTERVIEWING

The three most important aspects to interviewing are to know yourself, know the company, and know how you can benefit the company. Interviewing is seldom easy, but it will be easier for you since you have followd the steps and guidelines in this book. In preparing your resume, and in your job search process, you have been preparing yourself for the interview. By writing a functional resume, targeted toward a specific job goal, you have gained a good understanding of your skills, qualifications, and capabilities. You have practiced your interviewing skills by contacting people and organizations and discussing how your skills and interests match the company. The real interview will still make you nervous. However, if you know your capabilities and qualifications, and if you have thoroughly researched your field, you will have the confidence necessary for a successful interview. Some basic tactics of interviewing are:

Dress appropriately: If you do not know what that is, go to the company before your interview and see how they dress. However, a good rule of thumb, is for a man to wear slacks, a jacket and a tie, and for a woman to wear a dress or a suit. In most professional jobs, men should wear suits to interviews even when they will not wear them on the job. If you are applying for a job as a carpenter, you will not wear a suit, but will want to look neat and presentable.

Be conservative: The interviewers are getting their impression from meeting you only once or twice. When interviewing, first impressions do count. Women should tone down make up and hair styles. Men should be clean shaven (if you wear a beard or mustache, shave the area that you have not grown out) and get a hair cut. A lot has been written about colors to wear and not to wear, and how to dress. If you are unsure, pick up a book on interviewing, or attend a workshop in your community. Buy yourself one or two interviewing out fits and use them. If you buy yourself a suit (men and women) with a conservative cut, it will last you several years of interviewing, if that's what you need. Hopefully not.

Self-knowledge: Know how your skills and qualifications relate to the particular job requirements. Be specific. Don't say "I love to work with people." Explain your experience in guiding, directing, listening to or helping people. Cite some accomplishments.

Know your assets and liabilities: They may ask, so be prepared. Name your assets first and turn your liabilities into assets.

Have Job/Company knowledge: It shows enthusiasm and interest. Do your homework. Know the company's products or services, policies, problems with which you can help, and how your skills will benefit the company (not how the company can boost your career).

Confidence: Show your confidence and enthusiasm when talking about your experience and your interest in the company. Be sure, however, to listen carefully to the interviewers. Do not interrupt; answer their questions carefully. If you have an interviewer who tends to talk a lot and not ask a lot, interrupt at an appropriate time to discuss how your qualifications may fit into the company's needs.

Honesty: Answer the questions honestly. You want to get the job, but you do not want a job for which you are not qualified, or that does not fit you.

Persuasiveness: The trick is to assure the interviewers that you are the person for the job. Some people are just good salesmen. If you are not, your key is in your enthusiasm, interest and confidence in yourself. This comes with knowing yourself, and knowing the employers needs.

Personality: Aside from standard qualifications necessary for the job, the interviewers are also hiring a person. Therefore, the interviewers are looking for someone with whom they and other coworkers can get along. You should also assess whether your interviewers appear to be the type of people with whom you would like to work.

Do not smoke or chew gum: If you need a smoke, do it outside before you enter the building. Your prospective employer may prefer a non-smoker.

Be alert in the waiting area: The receptionist or secretary in the lounge may have input on hiring you. Often secretaries are asked about their impression of the candidate. They see you off your guard, and are able to form a good judgement. View this as an opportunity to converse casually with someone who is working for the company. You may learn more about the company. But don't use this as your last chance to find out about the company because you didn't do your homework. Show interest.

Remember names: When meeting your interviewer or interview panel remember their names. Do a rhyme game, or an association game to remember names. For instance John is blonde, or Linda, like your cousin with the same name.

Job Description: If you do not receive a job description early in the interview, ask about the job duties. It will help you in answering the interview questions. It will also help you determine if this is the job for you. It is best to get information about the particular job duties before you go into the interview, but if you were unable to get specifics, you should ask.

Questions: Have some. The depth of your questions will indicate how much you know about the job and company. Asking questions is an active role in the interview shows your interest. Do not bombard the interviewers with questions, however. Allow them to explain the job duties before you begin to ask. You may ask questions about salary and benefits, but don't let these appear to be your primary concern.

Salary: You should know the salary range for your particular position before the interview. You may get this information from personnel, or you may have a general idea of the going salary from your own research of the field. If you were unable to acquire specifics from the company before the interview, ask about a salary range during the interview. They may throw the question back at you and ask what you feel you are worth. In that case, know what you're worth. You should know the going rate for someone of your qualifications working in that type of position. There may be some negotiating at this point. Sometimes they are not presented until you are offered the job.

Shake hands: A firm handshake will be remembered.

Body Language: Eye contact shows confidence. Sit up straight and lean forward. Do not cross your legs. Be aware of your hands. If you tend to use them too much, or have a nervous habit, keep them in your lap.

Lighten up: Break the ice in the beginning of the interview by talking about something light, like something humorous in the paper. You may have a common interest with the interviewers. In a tense situation like an interview you may need some comic relief. But don't try to be a comedian.

Terminating the interview: The interviewers may give you an opportunity to say something at the end. If so, be prepared to give a summary of why you think you are the right person for the job and why you want to work for them in particular. If they don't, end the interview yourself with a hand shake, telling them how you have enjoyed the opportunity and why you think you would be good for the position. Find out when they will be making a decision, and who will be calling whom.

Thank you note: It's good etiquette. It is also an opportunity to highlight your skills.

TABLE 9 - JOB SEARCH RESOURCES

Chamber of Commerce Directories
College Alumni Associations
College Placement Offices
Community Centers Directories
Employment Agencies
Government Offices - Federal, State, County, City,
　　　School Districts
Internships
Interviews for Information
Job Listings
Networking
Newspaper Advertisements and Articles
Past Experience - Previous Employment
Periodicals
Professional Organizations
State Employment Office
Telephone Directories
Trade Associations
Unions
Volunteer Work

GENRAL RESOURCES

CAREER OPPORTUNITY INDEX

CAREER OPPORTUNITY UPDATE

ENCYCLOPEDIA OF ASSOCIATIONS - 1,200
associations

GUIDE TO AMERICAN DIRECTORIES - 5,000
directories in more than 200 fields

STANDARD RATE AND DATA - Names and
addresses of trade publications

(Continued)

TABLE 9 -Continued

HEALTH

    HUMAN SERVICE ORGANIZATIONS

    NATIONAL DIRECTORY OF PUBLIC SOCIAL AGENCIES

    PUBLIC WELFARE DIRECTORY

EDUCATION

    CALIFORNIA PRIVATE SCHOOL DIRECTORY

    DIRECTORY OF PUBLIC SCHOOLS IN THE U.S.

    EDUCATIONAL DIRECTORY

    TEACHING IN THE COMMUNITY-JUNIOR COLLEGE - American Association of Community and Junior Colleges

GOVERNMENT

    CAREERS IN CALIFORNIA STATE GOVERNMENT - California State Personnel Board

    FEDERAL CAREER DIRECTORY

    GUIDE TO FEDERAL CAREER LITERATURE - U.S. Office of Personnel Management

    WORKING FOR THE U.S.A. - U.S. Office of Personnel Management

(Continued)

TABLE 9 - Continued

GENERAL BUSINESS

AMERICA'S CORPORATE FAMILIES AND
INTERNATIONAL AFFILIATES -
Address, phone number, telex, major product or service, chief
operating officer.

BUSINESS INDEX - Microfilm; updated monthly;
400 business periodicals

BUSINESS PERIODICAL INDEX - Basic starting point. Covers 350 English
language business journals.

DIRECTORY OF CORPORATE AFFILIATIONS AND AMERICA'S
CORPORATE FAMILIES AND INTERNATIONAL AFFILIATES - Address,
phone number and chief operating officer.

DUN AND BRADSTREET MILLION DOLLAR DIRECTORY - Companies
with net worth between one-half and one million.

DUN AND BRADSTREET REFERENCE BOOK OF CORPORATE
MANAGEMENT - Background on directors of companies.

NEW YORK TIMES INDEX - Indexing of extensive financial
section of paper.

PRINCIPAL INTERNATIONAL BUSINESSES - Address, phone number,
telex, major product or service, chief operating officer of foreign owned
companies.

READER'S GUIDE TO PERIODICALS - Articles by topic.

STANDARD AND POOR'S INDUSTRY SURVEYS - Basic data and financial
outlook for 25 major industries.

(Continued)

TABLE 9 - Continued

STANDARD AND POOR'S REGISTER OF CORPORATIONS, DIRECTORS AND EXECUTIVES - Biographical information on top executives.

STANDARD DIRECTORY OF ADVERTISERS AND SUPPLEMENTS - 17,000 companies doing national and regional advertising.

THOMAS REGISTER OF AMERICAN MANUFACTURERS - Large and small product manufaturers.

TRADE NAMES DIRECTORY, GALE RESEARCH COMPANY - Guide to nearly 200,000 trade, brand, product amd design names.

U.S. INDUSTRIAL OUTLOOK, U.S. GOVERNMENT PRINTING OFFICE - Annual survey of current trends and outlook for more than 200 industries.

WALL STREET JOURNEL INDEX - Indexes on monthly basis.

WARD'S BUSINESS DIRECTORY - Information on privately owned companies.

WHO'S WHO IN FINANCE AND INDUSTRY - Biographical information on top executives.

WORLD DIRECTORY OF MULTINATIONAL ENTERPRISES, GALE RESEARCH CO. - Profiles 500 multinational industrial corporations.

TABLE 10 - TYPICAL INTERVIEW QUESTIONS

SELF (PERSONAL SKILLS/PREFERENCES):

1. Tell me about yourself.
2. Why did you choose your particular field of work?
3. What do you think determines a person's progress in a good company?
4. What personal characteristics are necessary for success in your chosen field?
5. Do you prefer working with others or by yourself?
6. What jobs have you enjoyed the most? The least?
7. What have you done to show initiative and willingness to work?
8. What type of boss do you prefer?
9. What are your strengths and weaknesses?
10. Why should we hire you rather than someone else for this job?

EXPERIENCE, SKILLS, GOALS:

1. What qualifications do you have that would make you successful in this field?
2. What do you know about opportunities in this field?
3. What would you do if...(situation testing technical knowledge or interactive skills)?
4. What is your career goal?
5. Have you plans to return to school?
6. Where do you see yourself in five years? Ten years?
7. What jobs have you held?

COMPANY:

1. What do you know about our company?
2. What do you know about this position?

(Continued)

TABLE 10 - Continued

3.   Why do you want to work for us?
4.   In what type of position are you most interested?
5.   Why do you think you would like this particular job?
6.   How long do you expect to work in this job?

MISCELLANEOUS:

1.   What salary requirements do you have?
2.   Can you get recommendations from previous employers?
3.   Are you willing to relocate? Travel? Work overtime? Weekends? Nights?

TABLE 11 - QUESTIONS TO ASK OF THE INTERVIEWER(S)

1. Can you tell me what a typical day would be like?

2   What are the responsibilities of this position?

3. Can you describe the typical career pattern of someone entering this position?

4. Can I progress at my own speed or is it structured?

5. What is the firm's policy with regard to paying for educational fees and expenses?

6. How often are performance reviews given?

7. Does this firm promote from within?

8. What is the salary range for this position?

9. Can you describe the hours, overtime, travel, relocation, benefits, etc.?

10. When will you make a decision? May I call . . .?

TABLE 12A - INTERVIEWER'S CHECKLIST

SKILLS:

Communication - listens, verbal, written, clear and concise.

Interpersonal - sensitive, independent, mature, assertive.

Persuasive - convincing.

Decision Making - objective, judgement, decisive.

Organization and Planning - sets priorities, plans actions, allocates resources.

KNOWLEDGE:

Self-Awareness - strengths vs weaknesses, personal goals, needs, expectations.

Experience - education, technical, professional knowledge.

Intellectual - analytical, creative, learning and reasoning ability.

Organizational - Understands position's responsibilities within organization.

ATTITUDE:

Initiative - takes on new projects/ responsibilities.

Tenacity - can-do approach to problems, opportunities.

Flexible - adaptable toward positions, company, overtime.

Team player - positive working relations.

Supervision - minimum guidance or structure.

(Continued)

TABLE 12A - Continued

WORK ETHIC:

Honesty, integrity

Achievement oriented.

Reliable, consistent.

Growth oriented, seeks new challenges.

TABLE 12B - INTERVIEWER'S CHECKLIST DEFINITIONS

Analytical Ability: The extent to which one is able to carefully and critically examine materials and situations, identify the problem and alternatives to consider in dealing with issues.

Communication: The extent to which the individual expresses himself both orally and in written work, presenting his ideas concisely, clearly and persuasively using appropriate format and grammar.

Decisiveness: The ability to have and give a clear result; settling something beyond doubt.

Flexibility: Being able to adapt oneself to change or situations if another's position is more correct.

Interpersonal Sensitivity: Being aware of and concerned about other human beings in their relationships to each other in a social environment, and the ability to respond to the needs, interests and capabilities of others.

Judgement: The ability to make up one's mind about what to do and do it, and to form opinions and show good sense and fair-minded in so doing.

Leadership: The extent to which an individual effectively directs the behavior of others to accomplish a task or goal without arousing hostility.

Management Role Identification: The extent to which an individual understands the supervisory/management role and the ability to adapt willingly and comfortably to it.

Organizing/Planning: The ability to anticipate future possibilities or consequences and work out a scheme of action, assembling information, materials, thoughts, or actions into a coherent, orderly logical unity.

Resistant to Stress: The extent to which an individual's performance stands up under stress.

Self-Confidence: Belief in one's own ability, power, and judgement.

Self-Control: Control of one's actions or feelings.

Technical Awareness: The ability to demonstrate a working knowledge of the basic fundamentals of one's chosen vocation. Being aware of current trends in one's professional field.

TABLE 13 - ILLEGAL INTERVIEW QUESTIONS

Name

Origin of name?

Maiden name?

Citizenship

Are you a U.S. citizen?

What country are you a citizen of?

Birthplace of applicant?

Of parents, relatives?

Birth certificate, naturalization?

National Origin

Ancestry, descent, nationality?

What languages do you speak?

What is your mother tongue?

Religion

Religious affiliation?

What holidays do you observe?

Age & Family Information

Birth date?

How old are you?

Are you married?

Do you have children?

Do you have childcare provisions?

SMITH FAMILY

EPILOG

Five years later ...

MARY:

Mary worked as a reporter on the college paper in her Sophomore year. It was a good experience for her, but she decided not to continue because she wanted to prepare for a study-abroad program in Venezuela. She decided on a major in comparative literature, spent her summer between her Sophomore and Junior year in an intensive Spanish program, and spent the second half of her Junior year, and summer in Venezuela. She is now fluent in Spanish and teaches English at a school in Lima, Peru. She has met other English teachers who have worked in Japan, and is investigating opportunities for herself there. She knows that she will eventually return to complete a graduate program, but is unsure if she will pursue writing, or continue with teaching.

SEAN:

Sean took the management position at the Stereo Store. The upper management was enthusiastic about his performance, and promised him more advancement opportunity within the corporate office once he completed his education. Excellent negotiator that he was, Sean agreed, providing that the company allow him to stay in his position, while cutting his hours by a third, and also pay for his education. He completed his B.S. in Business Management. Currently he works as an Operations Manager at the Stereo Place.

(Continued)

SMITH FAMILY - Continued

ANNE:

Anne completed courses that prepared her for a real estate license. She also researched alternative schools and found one that would accept several units for her traveling experience and knowledge of art history. With her previous college experience, and these extra units, she only had 40 semester units left to complete her B.A. degree in Humanities with an emphasis on Art History. Management positions in the antique business were scarce and did not pay enough for Anne's liking. She continued to dabble in antiques on her own, and worked for a real estate company. She did well enough to satisfy her pocket book, and traveled with her daughter through South America. Through her work, Anne met several people interested in purchasing antiques, hence she developed a small side business. She still does both jobs, but plans to slowly phase out the real estate work.

MIKE:

Unable to make a decision one way or another, Mike stayed in his job. He did take time off two summers in a row to visit places he always wanted to visit. He went with Anne to see their daughter, and took a detour, alone, to the Galapogos. He also joined the Sierra Club and frequently takes shorter trips. He has met several others with common interests, and through these networks found part-time employment as a Nest and Hack Site Attendant where he observes predatory birds. Although it is a non-paid activity, his involvement has grown. He is, again, considering the graduate degree. Mike has also advertised for a job partner to share his position as a Planner. Currently, Mike and Anne are discussing the financial possibility of him working part-time and returning to school.